CONTENTS

Nick Arnold has been writing stories and books since he was a youngster, but never dreamt he'd find fame writing about Fatal Forces. His research involved falling off buildings, lying on a bed of nails and skiing uphill and he enjoyed every minute of it.

When he's not delving into Horrible Science, he spends his spare time eating pizza, riding his bike and thinking up corny jokes (though not all at the same time).

www.nickarnold-website.com

Tony De Saulles picked up his crayons when he was still in nappies and has been doodling ever since. He takes Horrible Science very seriously and even agreed to to test what happens when your parachute doesn't open. Fortunately, his injuries weren't too serious. When he's not out with his sketchpad, Tony likes to write poetry and play squash, though he hasn't written any poetry about squash yet.

www.tonydesaulles.co.uk

INTRODUCTION

Science has one fatal flaw. It can be *seriously* boring. Ask a simple question and you're forced to listen to a really boring, complicated answer.

* English translations:
1 Gravity is the force that pulls things down towards the Earth. The same force pulls a smaller object towards a much larger object.

And some answers have masses of mysterious mathematics…

And don't try arguing with a scientist either…

Or you'll get a forceful reply…

2 Gravity makes the ball speed up as it falls. This depends on the mass (amount of material) in the Earth and your distance from the Earth's centre.

3 You're asking too many questions. I'll try blinding you with science.

See what I mean? It's enough to make you die of boredom. Now that *would* be fatal.

So what are these laws? And what happens if you break them? Do you get expelled? Or perhaps there's a *really horrible* punishment in store for you. Maybe you'll be *forced* to endure extra science lessons with megatons of homework? And who *forces* you to obey these horrible laws anyway? Teachers? No.

WELL WHAT'S FORCING ME TO FALL, THEN?

Forces force you. Because forces force things to move. And a force can be anything from you flicking a pea, to the awesome gravity of a giant star. So the effects of forces can be an inter-galactic explosion or the pea ending up in your teacher's ear-hole. (This might cause an explosion too!)

But forces can have fascinating fatal effects. Like crushing people, or making them sick, or pulling their heads off. (Getting forces wrong at school isn't usually quite as fatal — just a bit of en-forced detention from your teacher.)

So here's the real-life story of forces. It's a story involving fatal fortunes and horrible happenings. And it's all true. And who knows? Afterwards you might feel that forces have a fatal attraction for you, too. You might even force your teacher to take your science homework seriously. If you can just force yourself to read the next page now…

NASTY NEWTON

The prisoner was sick. In the madness of his fever he imagined the courtroom candles were fiery ghosts. Again and again he heard the sentence of the judges: "Death!" Then he fainted.

He awoke in darkness. Dragging himself upright he tried to explore the pitch-black cell. His feet slithered on the slimy floor. Then he stumbled, his hands grabbing at empty air. He'd collapsed on the edge of a bottomless pit. One more step and he'd have dropped like a stone. Exhausted, the prisoner fell asleep. But when he awoke he found himself strapped to a low bench. Helpless, he peered upwards and gasped in horror.

A giant statue towered over him. The grotesque figure had a huge pendulum swinging from its hands. The pendulum swung to and fro with an evil hiss. It ended in a razor-sharp blade and each slow sweep brought the blade a little lower. A little closer. Hiss … hiss … HISSSSSS! Scores of huge rats stared hungrily from the shadows, waiting to feast on the prisoner's butchered corpse. The deadly hissing blade skimmed his bare chest…

DON'T PANIC! It's only a story – *The Pit and the Pendulum* was written in 1843 by the American author Edgar Allan Poe. But for scientists Poe's story has a fatal fascination. The nasty forms of death – the pit and the pendulum – involve forces. Falling into the well under the influence of gravity; the pendulum's swing controlled by gravity and centripetal force (see page 130). (That's the force on the pendulum shaft that stops the swinging weight pulling away from the rest of the machine.) These forces are fatal for the prisoner.

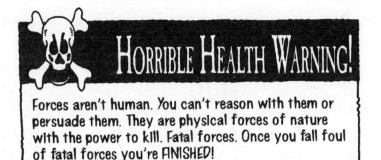

HORRIBLE HEALTH WARNING!

Forces aren't human. You can't reason with them or persuade them. They are physical forces of nature with the power to kill. Fatal forces. Once you fall foul of fatal forces you're FINISHED!

Postscript:
Oh – by the way you'll be pleased to know the prisoner escapes. How? By getting the rats to gnaw through his straps, of course. Bet you didn't think of that! Amazingly enough these forces had already been explained by a forceful scientific mega-star, the amazing Sir Isaac Newton.

Hall of fame: Sir Isaac Newton (1642–1727) **Nationality:** British

Isaac Newton was born on Christmas Day. The doctor thought baby Isaac wouldn't live because he was so weak and small. But Isaac survived. He soon became interested in science but his teachers didn't think he was especially brainy. In fact, Isaac was too busy performing experiments at home to work hard at school. (Don't try this excuse.) When young Isaac was 16 his mum asked him to run the family farm. But he proved to be a useless farmer. He spent all his time experimenting and allowed the sheep to guzzle their way through a cornfield.

So Isaac went to Cambridge University instead. At university he read every maths book he could find. (Including the ones without pictures.) He wore scruffy clothes and was so absent-minded he often got lost on his way to supper. As far as Isaac was concerned supper was for wimps. Who needed supper when you could do lovely science calculations instead?

In 1665 a deadly plague struck London. Soon 7,000 people were dying every week and the authorities closed Cambridge University to stop the plague spreading. So Isaac went home. But instead of taking a holiday he did *extra homework*. Very strange. But what homework! He invented calculus – a mathematical system still used today to plan rocket trips, and he also discovered that light contains colours.

These vital discoveries have influenced maths and science ever since. But then Isaac made a *really* incredible breakthrough. It may have happened like this...

THE APPLE AND THE MOON

Woolsthorpe, England 1666

It was getting dark, but the skinny young man ran his fingers through his shoulder-length hair and carried on reading. Isaac Newton was sitting in the orchard trying to figure out how the moon went round the Earth. Suddenly a call rang out from the old farmhouse:

"Isaac, your supper's ready!"

"Yes, mother."

"Hmm," thought Isaac, "she always calls me half an hour *before* supper. It's a trick to get me in on time."

So he did nothing. If he had left the orchard when his mother called him the entire history of science would have been different. But just then something grabbed his attention.

It had been waiting for this moment. Waiting for months, silently. At first it was no larger than a tiny green bulge. But now it was bright red and the size of a man's fist. A living bubble of water and sugars with sweet juicy flesh and bitter seeds all wrapped in a waxy skin. An apple. The most famous apple in science.

"Isaac! Your supper's on the table and it's your favourite!"

"Coming, mother!"

Isaac shivered as a cool breeze rustled the trees. Then he sighed and reluctantly closed his book. There was a silent snap. The slender stalk holding the apple to the tree gave way. Wrenched by an unseen force the apple hurtled downward. It tumbled through the rustling leaves and bounced with a crunch on Isaac's brainy bonce.

What would you have done? Perhaps you'd have eaten your supper and forgotten the apple. But Isaac wasn't like that. He rubbed his head and looked at the moon. It shone like a bright silver coin in the evening sky.

"So why doesn't the moon fall, too?" he asked himself, as he absent-mindedly munched the famous apple.

For some strange reason Isaac remembered his school and the dreaded "bucket game". He hated the other kids for making him play. He remembered having to whirl a bucket of water around his head on a rope. It was hard work and Isaac was a thin little boy.

But amazingly all the water had stayed in the bucket as if trapped by an unseen force.

"Maybe that's what keeps the moon in place," he murmured.

Then his mother shouted again: "Isaac, your supper's on the table and it's stone cold."

"I said I'm coming, mother!"

As Isaac threw the apple away he wondered what would happen if it reached the moon. The most famous apple core in science disappeared. There was a muffled meow as it splatted on the cat.

Isaac had forgotten his supper. He was calculating how strong gravity would need to be to stop the apple sailing into space. Then he thought about how fast the moon has to move to prevent it crashing down to Earth.

Later a very annoyed Mrs Newton stood in the doorway shielding her candle from the cold night air.

"Isaac!" she yelled. "I've fed your supper to the cat. And I'm going to feed your breakfast to the pigs!"

There was no answer from the orchard. But Isaac was still out there. And still thinking hard.

15

TEST YOUR TEACHER

How much does your teacher really know about this famous scientist?

1 As a child what was Isaac Newton's favourite toy?

a) A chemistry set.

b) A toy windmill powered by a mouse in a wheel.

c) He hated toys. He preferred tricky maths sums.

2 What did he buy on his first day at university?

a) A desk, ink and a notebook for extra homework.

b) New clothes and a ticket to the local fun fair.

c) A loaf of bread to eat.

3 How did Newton solve tricky scientific problems?

a) The answers came in a flash of inspiration when Newton was on the toilet.

b) By talking things over with scientific friends.

c) Worrying away at the problem day and night until he figured out the answer.

4 Newton became Professor of Mathematics at Cambridge but no one attended his bum-numbingly boring lectures. So what did he do?
a) He rounded up students and forced them to listen.
b) Carried on talking to an empty room.
c) Tried to make his lectures interesting with a few jokes and amusing stories.

5 Newton's dog, Diamond, knocked over a candle and years of hard work went up in flames. What did he do?
a) Drew his sword and killed the dog.
b) Re-wrote his work from memory.
c) He told the dog off and went on to study something new and experimental.

ANSWERS
1b) He designed it himself. 2a), 3c), 4b) Does your teacher have this problem? 5b).

NEWTON'S MOVING BOOK

Newton didn't publish his discoveries for 20 years. He was too busy with his mathematical work. But then at last, fearful others might grab the glory, Newton wrote a book about his ideas. He shut himself away for 18 months and worked 20 hours a day.

Sometimes Newton's assistant reminded him that he'd missed supper.

"Have I?" Newton would murmur sleepily. Then he nibbled at the food and got back to work.

THE CARROT WAS FOR YOUR SUPPER, SIR

Newton's book was called *The Philosophiæ Naturalis Principia Mathematica* and it was the most brilliant science book ever written. In it he explained the whole universe in a way that made sense. (Well – it would have made sense if the book hadn't been in Latin and filled with mystifying maths.) Newton described gravity and three crucial laws about forces and how things move. These laws show how squids squirt water backwards in order to move forwards. They explain what happens when distant stars blow up and why low-flying sparrow droppings splat on your head.

One way to imagine Newton's laws is to think of a really horrible morning. What d'you mean – every day's like that?

Newton's First Law

What the law says...
If left alone, a motionless object..✳..
doesn't move. A moving object carries
on moving in a straight line at a
constant speed as long as another
force doesn't make it change course.

What the Law means...

You stare wearily at your breakfast. Your cornflakes are motionless and they're going to stay that way until you summon up the energy to eat them. You clumsily knock your spoon and half your breakfast goes flying. A cornflake falls on your dad's head. The cornflake would have flown in the same direction for ever but the force of gravity pulled it down.

Newton's Second Law

what the law says...
A force changes an object's speed. The change in speed is proportional to the strength of the force. The change in speed happens in the direction of the force.

What the Law means…

The harder you kick a ball, the faster it flies in that direction. It's a rotten result for a goalie!

Newton's Third Law

> *What the law says…*
> *When an object exerts a force on another object the second object will push back just as hard.*

What the Law means …

You're late and you're jogging to school. But you're still not properly awake. You slam into a lamppost. And the lamppost wallops you back! It's true – this really does happen.

OUCH!

WHAM

BET YOU NEVER KNEW!

When Newton's apple hit the ground, the Earth bumped against the apple. That's what Newton's Third Law says: things always push back with equal force. But the Earth moved such a tiny distance no one noticed. Oddly enough a unit of force was later named the "Newton" in the scientist's honour. And the weight produced by one Newton is roughly the same as ... an apple. But Newton was no ordinary genius. He had a nasty side, too.

NEWTON'S NASTY NATURE

1 When Newton was three years old his mum remarried. Isaac hated his stepfather and often thought of killing him. He didn't, of course, but he was pleased when the stepfather died.

2 At school Newton had no friends until he thumped the school bully with great force. Newton was smaller than his opponent but his courage helped win the fight. After this nasty incident Newton became popular.

3 Newton disliked women and never married. He hated his friend John Locke's attempts to introduce him to ladies. Later Newton wrote to Locke:

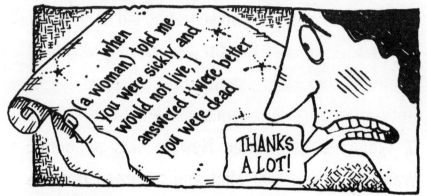

But that didn't stop Newton generously allowing his niece Catherine to do his cooking and cleaning.

4 Newton was a miserable man. He had no hobbies apart from work. He rarely laughed and he called poetry: "A kind of ingenious nonsense."

5 In 1686 Newton fell out with scientist Robert Hooke (1635–1703). Hooke unjustly accused Newton of pinching *his* ideas on gravity. In a letter

Newton called Hooke "a pretender and a grasper" and refused to talk to him.

6 After writing the *Principia,* Newton had a nasty turn. He went mad for two years and did no scientific research. Some historians reckon Newton was a bit depressed but others say he was poisoned by the mercury he used for chemistry experiments.

7 When he got better, Newton was appointed Warden of the Royal Mint and reformed Britain's coinage. It was said that nasty Newton enjoyed catching forgers and arranging especially nasty executions for them.

8 German Gottfried Leibniz (1646–1716) claimed he invented calculus. Newton accused Leibniz of pinching his idea. But in fact Leibniz had made the discovery independently at the same time as Newton. (And it was Leibniz who actually coined the word "calculus" – Newton called it "fluxions" – which sounds like the effects of a nasty tummy bug.)

9 Newton came to a horrible end. He moved to the country to improve his health. But a few weeks later he fell sick and died of a stone in his bladder. By then, however, he was a nasty-tempered old man of 84, but still a great genius.

NEWTON IN HIS OWN WORDS

Like many geniuses, Newton was hard to understand. Here's what he said about himself:

He also said: "I seem to have been only a boy playing on the seashore … whilst the great ocean of truth lay all undiscovered before me." **

There are loads more fatally fascinating facts about forces. You'll find them in the next chapter.

* Newton didn't mean human pyramids. The giants he referred to were earlier scientists who inspired him.

** Newton meant that he'd learnt enough to realize there was more to learn. He was right. He'd only scratched the surface.

FORCEFUL FACTS

Forces are *everywhere*. You can't do much without bumping into them. But hopefully not with a fatal *CRUNCH*. Oddly enough, though, before Newton, people knew very little about how forces worked.

MIXED-UP MOTION THEORIES

A scientist will tell you that a force is something that affects the movement or shape of an object or person. Sounds fairly vague. But before Newton, scientific theories were even more mixed-up. One of the first people to write about forces was a Greek genius called Aristotle.

Hall of fame: Aristotle (384–322 BC)

Nationality: Greek

Aristotle was a doctor's son. His parents died when he was a child and as a young man he blew their money on wild parties. But when he was 17 years old Aristotle had a sudden change of heart and sent himself back to school.

He went to study under the brainy philosopher called Plato in the Academy at Athens. Aristotle liked it there so much that he stayed for the next 20 years as a pupil and then as a teacher.

Aristotle travelled for four years and eventually moved to Macedonia where his old mate Philip happened to be king. Phil asked Aristotle to teach his boy, Alexander. Aristotle must have done a good job because young Alexander became Alexander the Great and conquered a great chunk of Asia. By the time Aristotle died (of acute indigestion) he had written about everything from politics to how grasshoppers chirp. And he even had a few things to say about forces.

Here's how Aristotle explained forces:

IT WANTS
TO HURRY
DOWN TO
EARTH – ITS
NATURAL
RESTING
PLACE.

THROB

EH?

Wrong, wrong and wrong again. But for 2,000 years everyone thought Aristotle's wacko ideas were RIGHT. Eventually Newton used maths to prove Aristotle WRONG. So nowadays we've got forces sussed. As a scientist might say, "Learning about forces is as easy as riding a bike." Oh, yeah? Riding a bike is LOADS harder and just to prove it we've asked a scientist to try.

SCIENTIFIC CYCLING IN TEN EASY LESSONS

LESSON 1: WOBBLY BALANCE

Remember learning to ride a bike? Tough, wasn't it? Inside the scientist's ears are fluid-filled spaces called semi-circular canals. (Teachers have a larger air-filled space where their brains should be. Ha ha.) These canals help her balance on two wheels. As the liquid sloshes around, sensors tell her brain whether she's still upright. Her brilliant brain also notices the force of gravity, her speed, the slope and wind direction. Yep — all at the same time.

THE SMALL PRINT:
IT'S NOT OUR FAULT IF YOU END UP IN HOSPITAL - OK?

It helps her balance if her science books, sandwiches, etc, aren't draped over one handlebar. Ideally her bum is the centre of gravity — the point around which everything else is sensibly balanced.

LESSON 2: EFFORTLESS INERTIA

When she stands still, inertia keeps her there. She overcomes inertia to get moving. Once she's moving, inertia keeps her going in a straight line. Mind you, she needs more pedal power to get up hills!

Larger objects have more inertia. That's why it's hard to stop a charging elephant. And if you're daft enough to try you might feel a bit flat afterwards!

OH DEAR! THE HILL SEEMS TO HAVE GOT A BIT STEEPER

PUFF! GASP!

HILLS REQUIRE MORE ENERGY

SCIENTIST HAS TO PUSH DOWN HARDER ON THE PEDALS

LESSON 3: MASS-IVE MOMENTUM
Momentum is a measure of the scientist's ability to keep going. And her momentum depends on her mass. If your reaction to this statement is to say "yer wot?", you'd better read the next bit. Mass means how much there is of the scientist — everything in her body, her clothes and even what she had

for breakfast. Her mass, her bike's mass and her speed combine to produce her momentum. Wheee!

LESSON 4: MIXED-UP MOMENTUM

Oops! She knocks the school bully flying. Scientists would say she's "transferred momentum" to the bully and call this "conserving momentum". The posh scientific word for speed in one direction is "velocity". So she'd better pedal at quite a velocity in order to conserve her life!

TRANSFER OF MOMENTUM TAKES PLACE HERE

BOO!

BULLY LANDS SOMEWHERE OVER HERE

BAD

Oo-er now the bully's heading towards her on a skateboard. THEY'RE GOING TO CRASH! As they crash the two momentums cancel each other. So they both grind to a halt. Result = TROUBLE!!!

LESSON 5: GALLOPING GRAVITY

Velocity is greater when cycling downhill. Gravity tries to pull the scientist to the centre of the Earth. And the bottom of the slope is a bit nearer the centre of the planet than the top. This explains why, if she loses her balance, it's easier to fall off her bike than

stay on. By the way, if she did make
it right through to the Earth's
centre, there would be no gravity
and she would float around being
roasted in the fiery heat. Not nice!
Tired yet? Our scientist is. She's
run out of kinetic energy. That's
the posh scientific name for the
energy she uses when moving. Oh well
— we'll give her a few minutes to
recover and then we'll put her back
to work.

LESSON 6: AWKWARD
ACCELERATION AND DRAG
For the scientist the word
"acceleration" means changing speed
or direction. So even when she slows

down, she calls it "acceleration". But when she accelerates down a hill she feels the wind whistling up her nostrils (and everywhere else), and trying to slow her. This force is called "drag". If it's particularly windy it'll "drag" her off her bike — the result could be fatal.

WIND BLOWS AGAINST THE SCIENTIST AND CAUSES "DRAG" WHICH SLOWS HER DOWN

CROUCHING DOWN REDUCES THE DRAG AND HELPS HER TO GO FASTER!

LESSON 7: CURIOUS CORNERING

As the scientist rounds the corner, centripetal (sen-tre-pee-tal) force pulls her bike into the corner. But her inertia opposes the change in course. It tries to keep her moving in a straight line (remember Newton's First Law?). The scientist feels as if a force is pushing her outwards. As a scientist she knows this isn't a real force — it's all in her imagination!

SCIENTIST LEANS THIS WAY →

TO COUNTER-BALANCE HER MOMENTUM ←

LESSON 8: GRINDING GEARS

The gears on the scientist's bike help her cycle uphill. The gears allow her to pedal quicker but with less force. This means she can cycle up the slope without getting puffed out. Yep — gears are great. As a scientist would say, "They're a great way of transferring forces."

LESSON 9: FURIOUS FRICTION

The force of friction slows moving objects. It happens when a moving object touches another object. The scientist's rubber tyres grip the road and provide this force. This helps her control the bike and avoid fatal collisions. Lack of friction makes cycling on ice a slippery experience. And performing wheelies on the local skating rink is definitely out.

When she wants to slow down or stop, the rubber brakes grip her wheels. Friction stops her bike. Hopefully. If she brakes too hard, her momentum throws her forward. And she performs spectacular but possibly fatal handlebar acrobatics.

LESSON 10: VICIOUS VIBRATIONS

When the scientist rides her bike along a bumpy path she may feel a few vibrations. These are shock waves carrying the force of impact from the tyres. Her tyres and saddle springs are designed to soak up some vibrations. But that doesn't stop her body vibrating, her muscles twitching and her eyeballs bouncing slightly in their sockets.

FREAKY PHYSICISTS

Scientists who study forces are called physicists (*fizzy-sists*). They also explore motion, probe what things are made of, and try to figure out how the universe works. A typical physicist is slightly scruffy and enjoys tinkering with things. A physics lab is rather untidy and full of interesting bits and pieces that have been salvaged in order to build a freaky machine.

FATAL EXPRESSIONS

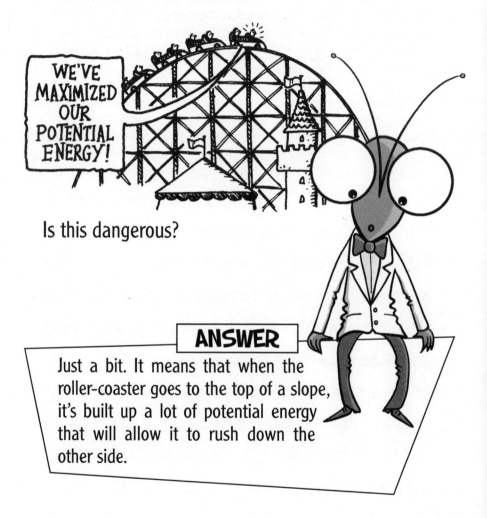

Is this dangerous?

ANSWER

Just a bit. It means that when the roller-coaster goes to the top of a slope, it's built up a lot of potential energy that will allow it to rush down the other side.

BET YOU NEVER KNEW!

Physicists use two strange words in connection with forces – "energy" and "work". Well hopefully, they don't sound too strange to you. But we're not talking about summoning up the energy to do homework or wash the dishes here. No way.

Physicists say "work" when they want to explain what happens when a force causes an object to move a distance. According to them writing your maths homework is "work" but reckoning up the answers in your head isn't. Energy is the ability to do work. Sounds sensible – after all you need energy to work. Don't you?

Just thinking about energy and work is pretty exhausting isn't it, so why don't you take a little rest? Yeah – put your feet up. Get your breath back for the next chapter. You'll need it. 'Cos it's about speed and crashes!!! Fasten your seat belt.

SMASHING SPEED

Some people think speed is smashing. Others don't. Early railways scared some people because they reckoned no human could go faster than 32 km per hour (20 mph) and live. Well, they can, of course. But one thing's certain – the faster you go the more likely you are to meet up with some fatal forces. Gulp!

TEST YOUR TEACHER

Is your teacher quick-witted? Smile sweetly and ask:

WHAT WAS THE FASTEST SPEED ATTAINED ON A BICYCLE DURING THE NINETEENTH CENTURY?

(Note the subtle wording — your teacher probably thinks you're talking about pedalling — but she'd be wrong.)

Your teacher will probably say something like, "50 km per hour" (31 mph) — hopelessly wrong. At this point you can say, "No, I think you're wrong. In 1899 Mr C M Murphy smashed the record. He tied his bike to the back of a train and travelled 1.6 km in a minute." DON'T try this at home.

QUICK QUIZ

1 Super speedy

See if you can put these three objects in order of speed, starting with the fastest.

a) A bullet from a high-powered rifle.

b) The planet Mercury moving through space.

c) Three astronauts aboard the Apollo 10 spacecraft in 1969.

2 Fairly speedy

Which of these three objects do you think is the fastest?

a) A chameleon's tongue as it grabs a juicy fly.

b) A message sent along one of your nerves.

c) A person falling from the top of a 99.4-metre-high building.

3 Slow and sluggish

Can you put these three objects in order of speed starting with the fastest?

a) Your fingernails growing.

b) Bamboo plants growing.

c) The Atlantic Ocean getting wider.

1b) 172,248 km per hour (107,030 mph) When it comes to orbiting the sun, Mercury is the speediest planet in the solar system. **c)** 39,897 km per hour (24,791 mph) Feeling a teensy bit space sick? **a)** 3,302 km per hour (2,052 mph). That's too fast to see. The bullet travels faster than sound so a person could be shot before they heard the gun firing. Doesn't sound fair somehow.

2b) Up to 483 km per hour (300 mph). **c)** 141 km per hour (80 mph). This was the speed achieved by stuntman Dan Koko in 1984 as he leapt off the Las Vegas World Hotel. Lucky for Dan he smashed into an air cushion rather than the pavement. **a)** 80.5 km per hour (50 mph). Then it's bye-bye fly.

3b) 3 cm (1.2 inches) an hour. If your fingernails grew as fast as this, you'd have problems. **c)** 0.0006 cm (0.0002 inch) an hour. The Atlantic Ocean is getting wider due to the movements of enormous slabs of rock deep beneath the Earth's surface. **a)** 0.00028 cm (0.0001 inch) an hour. Any faster than this and it could be fatal.

BET YOU NEVER KNEW!

You'd move faster if your shape allowed the air to flow round you rather than bumping into you. This kind of shape is called "aerodynamic" and it cuts down on drag. A bullet with its pointed head is an aerodynamic shape but a human head isn't. If it was we'd all have pointy heads. Record-smashing speed cyclists wear pointed helmets instead. And more speed means more momentum. Smashing!

Fatal forces fact file

Name: Momentum

The basic facts: Momentum keeps you moving. That way you don't smash Newton's First Law. (That's the one about you going in a straight line unless something stops you.)

The horrible details: Momentum makes your stomach jump when you go over the top on a roller coaster. The momentum of your half-digested food carries on up. If it comes up too far it could be fatally embarrassing!

MURDEROUS MOMENTUM FACTS

1 In 1871 showman John Holtum tried to catch a flying cannon-ball *with his bare hands*. It wasn't fired from a real cannon, of course. Holtum used a specially built gun that fired a slow-moving ball. But even so he nearly lost a finger. The stunt proved very popular and John bravely practised until he'd perfected the trick. He should have changed his name to "Halt-em".

2 In nineteenth-century America railways were rarely fenced off and brainless buffalo often blundered onto the tracks. To tackle this menace, by the 1860s trains were fitted with wedge-shaped "cow catchers". The idea was that the train's momentum would scoop the buffalo out of harm's way.

3 In Finland, elk (otherwise known as moose) cause fatal road accidents. When hit by a car, the momentum of the car flips the moose over. So the loose moose lands on the car roof. Its weight crushes both the car and its driver. Perhaps the cars should be fitted with "moose catchers".

IDLE INERTIA

Physicists use the word inertia to describe how things stay the same. Motionless things stay idle and moving things carry on until another force gets in the way. That's Newton's First Law again.

DARE YOU DISCOVER ... THE INERTIA OF AN EGG?

You will need:
- A plate
- A raw egg
- A hard-boiled egg

What you do:

1 Gently spin the raw egg on the plate.

2 To stop the egg touch it with your finger.

3 Gently lift your finger up.

4 Now repeat steps 1–3 with the hard-boiled egg.

What do you notice?

a) When you lift your finger the hard-boiled egg continues to spin.

b) When you lift your finger the raw egg continues to spin.

c) When you lift your finger the raw egg spins and the hard-boiled egg rocks from end-to-end.

WHOOPS

DON'T PUSH
DOWN
TOO HARD

A SMASHING TEST

Car designers spend fortunes building new cars. And then they smash them up. This may sound stupid, but they need to test the car's structural design and materials under crash conditions and also find the best ways to ensure that the driver and passengers are as well protected as possible. These days most smashes happen on a computer screen. The engineers peer at a simulation of crashes at various speeds. They can even slow down the movement to one image every two milliseconds – that's far slower than a TV action replay.

But afterwards the engineers need real-life tests to check their findings. And this is when the poor old dummies get wheeled in to show the effects of the crash on real people. Of course, dummies don't have brains – that's why they're dummies. But they do have a smashing time.

A DAY IN THE LIFE OF A CRASH TEST DUMMY

11 am The crash test dummies arrive on a trolley and have to be helped into their car. There's a mum, a dad and two young dummies.

The car is wired up with all kinds of sensors plugged into it and it's facing the direction they'll be travelling ... straight into a wall! What's more, the engineers seem to have forgotten to fasten all four seat belts.

HAVE A NICE CRASH, DUMMIES!

<u>11.02 am</u> The engineers crouch behind steel barriers to protect themselves from the impact of the crash, and it turns out they *deliberately* forgot about the seat belts. Steel cables at the front of the car catapult it forward at speed. CRAACK! the car hits the wall. The dummies crash through the windscreen. The front of the car is completely smashed in.

12.00 noon
The dummies are cut free from the wreckage. They're a little bit battered but they've survived to crash another day. They're pretty tough dummies.

1.00pm
The engineers stop for a sandwich. The dummies aren't all that hungry.

SUIT YOURSELF!

2.00 pm Telly time! The dummies have become movie stars, but they don't even know it. As the dummies are wheeled away, the engineers settle themselves in front of a screen to watch an action replay of the crash on video.

You can see how Newton's First Law affects the dummies. That's the law about things continuing to move in a straight line. When the car stops, the inertia of the dummies forces

TERRIFIC!

SUPER!

them to carry on moving – straight through the windscreen. So the force of the wall hitting the car is transferred to the poor old dummies. You can see why seat belts are lifesavers. You'd be a real dummy not to wear one.

5.00 pm The engineers set up tomorrow's test. This time the dummies will be trapped in a car as it rolls over in a crash. But that's just another smashing day in the life of the crash test dummies.

A dummy's life is full of hard knocks.

Safety first

As a result of this testing, engineers have come up with a few ingenious devices to help reduce the impact of a car crash on passengers:

SCIENTIST'S CAR

Collapsible steering wheel: if the air bag fails, the steering wheel collapses rather than spearing the driver in the chest.

Airbags: if a driver is thrown forward onto the steering wheel of most modern cars, the bag inflates for a nice soft landing.

Seat belts soak up the force that throws the body forward.

Crumple zones: some parts of the car are designed to crumple in a crash. They soak up some of the force and divert it away from people in the car.

Side-impact bars strengthen the doors. The strong bars or tubes soak up some force if the car gets whacked from the side.

SMASHING SOUND SPEEDS

Fatal though they often are, the forces in a car crash are nothing compared to those in really high-speed accidents like an air crash. Or the horrible effects of falling out of an aeroplane at high speed. The effects of high speeds were studied by Austrian physicist Ernst Mach (1838–1916). Mach found that it's hard to travel faster than the speed of sound – 1,220 km per hour (760 mph). (By the way, the speed of sound is the speed sounds travel through the air.)

Here's why it's so difficult. All aircraft push air in front of them. But a plane flying at the speed of sound smashes into this air before it can escape. This makes for a violently bumpy ride that can shake the plane to pieces (not to mention your insides). In the 1940s several pilots died trying to smash the sound barrier. But in 1947 American pilot Charles E Yeager broke the barrier in a rocket-powered plane. It was known to be dangerous to fly really, really fast, but at this time no one knew what hitting the air at these speeds would do to an unprotected body. Could it be fatal?

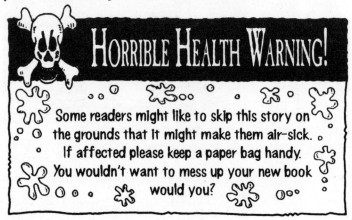

HORRIBLE HEALTH WARNING!

Some readers might like to skip this story on the grounds that it might make them air-sick. If affected please keep a paper bag handy. You wouldn't want to mess up your new book would you?

FLY FOR YOUR LIFE

26 February 1955, California, USA

At 9.30 am precisely, ace test pilot George Franklin Smith picked up his washing. He turned left out of the launderette and walked slap bang into the worst day of his life.

He should have known better. How many people volunteer

to work on a Saturday? But he had nothing better to do than finish a report. And of course when he got to work someone offered him a test flight in a gleaming brand new Super Sabre jet. This was a new type of jet plane capable of flying faster than sound.

George grinned. He loved test flying the powerful planes. In his laid-back way he replied:

YEAH, SURE I'LL TAKE HER UP. WON'T TAKE MORE THAN FORTY-FIVE MINUTES OR SO.

It wasn't worth putting on a protective suit.

As George took off he noticed the controls were a bit stiff. But there seemed nothing to worry about – the pre-flight checks had been just fine. He chatted happily to a pilot friend over the intercom.

Minutes later he broke the sound barrier. Then the plane nosed down and the controls jammed. The jet was diving to destruction at supersonic speed.

As his speed increased George yelled: "Controls locked – I'm going straight down!"

His friend's voice exploded in the headphones. "Bale out, George! Get out of there!" He had seconds to escape or die.

About 2,100 metres below, the blue sea glittered in the sunshine.

George wrenched the armrest and jettisoned the jet's perspex canopy. A tearing gale filled the cockpit. At this speed the violent force of the air pinned him down. He painfully stretched out his hand. His fingertips brushed the ejector seat handle. There was no time. No time to think of the danger. *Every* pilot who had baled out at supersonic speeds had been killed.

George's straining fingers clutched the handle. *KERBAAAM!* A powerful explosion tore him from the cockpit. He hit a wall of air. The world and the sky tumbled crazily. In a few seconds his shoes and socks, his watch and helmet were torn away. He was bleeding fast and very, very scared.

His falling body felt like a feather. "A falling body" he thought vaguely, "has no weight – it's … something to do with gravity." There was a crack and a sharp jerk as the parachute opened, its canopy trapping and slowing the air as it rushed past. Then George felt himself slip into darkness. He felt no pain as his body slammed into the sea and began to sink.

"Hey, give me a hand!" shouted the fisherman to his friend as he hauled the heavy body from the water.

The other man looked doubtful. "There's no point – I think the pilot's dead."

But George Smith was still alive. Just…

It took the Air Force a month to scoop up all the mangled pieces of George's plane from the sea bed 1.6 km from the shore. The wreckage filled 50 barrels and still no one knew what had caused the crash.

But scientists now had a chance to study the effect of extreme forces … on poor George's half-dead body.

Here's what they found out:

1 As George ejected from the plane, his speed boosted the effects of gravity. What we call "weight" depends on the strength of the gravity affecting our bodies. So every part of the pilot's body became 40 times heavier. You may have felt this yourself. It's that weird feeling of being stuck to your seat as you climb a roller-coaster. Only George was moving much faster so this effect was almost fatal.

2 Even his blood became heavier for a few moments. Heavy blood squirted from his heavy blood vessels. This caused a mass of bruises to appear on his body. He was so bruised that his head swelled up like a purple football.

3 George's eyelids bled after fluttering violently in the howling wind as he fell at speed.

In all George spent seven months in hospital. But he made a full recovery and went back to flying. He was the luckiest pilot in the world. Of course, every pilot's worst nightmare is to fall out of the sky. Because falling – under the influence of gravity – can be fatal. So if you want to survive the next chapter you'd better hang on tight. And DON'T FORGET YOUR PARACHUTE!

GRUESOME GRAVITY

What goes up must come down. This old saying is true as long as you're not in outer space where things float around all the time and don't "come down". Why? Because the further you get from a planet, the weaker its gravity becomes. So what is this unearthly force? Read on for the full and gruesome details.

Fatal forces fact file

Name: Gravity

The basic facts: You'll find gravity between any two things. Somehow they tug on each other. This effect is usually slight and you won't notice it unless one object is MASSIVE.

SMALLTHING

BIG THING
(THE EARTH)

The horrible details: Scientists think gravity is carried by tiny particles called gravitons and when an object accelerates it gives out gravity waves. The force of gravity has been used for some horrible executions (see page 68). In fact, whenever you fall, gravity brings you down to Earth with a bump.

TERMINAL VELOCITY

How's this for a thrill? You go for a flight in a plane up to, say, 6,100 metres and then you jump out. And you don't use a parachute. Well – not until you've fallen halfway to the ground under the influence of gravity. Is this completely crazy? No, it's a popular sport called freefall parachuting. If you don't mind heights and enjoy a bit of danger you'll love this. If not, you'd better put on a blindfold before you read this next bit.

65

HOW TO BE A FREEFALL
PARACHUTIST IN ONE QUICK LESSON

<u>1</u> Try not to look at the ground.
Jump out of the plane.

<u>2</u> Check your parachute is strapped
securely to your back. (Come to think
of it, that should have been Step 1.)

<u>3</u> Start tumbling. That's not
something you've got to do — it's
something that will happen to you
anyway. You'll find your sense of
balance can't help you stay upright.
You'll feel sick. Try not to panic
at this stage.

<u>4</u> For 15 seconds you fall faster and
faster. Every second you fall 9.8 metres
faster until you hit 50 metres a second
(100—150 mph). That's the maximum speed
you can fall. It's called terminal
velocity. Gulp! It's horrible feeling
there's nothing under you except
empty air, but some people can't get
enough of it.

<u>5</u> Good news. You won't fall any
faster because the air slows you
down — this force is known as drag.

<u>6</u> Here's your chance to practise
your freefall parachuting technique.
Try to fall face downwards. Spread
your arms and legs and stick your

stomach out. You'll find your body curves forwards and your arms and legs are pushed backwards. This makes a larger area for the drag to act upon. So you don't fall quite so fast. Flying squirrels and sky-diving cats do this in mid-air.

<u>7</u> One minute later. Had fun? Good. You're going to hit the ground in 25 seconds. Better pull your parachute rip cord now or you'll really fall foul of gravity. And make a rather deep hole in the ground.
<u>8</u> As you land, make sure you drop down to a squatting position. Bending your knees soaks up some force as you hit the ground. Enjoyed it? Great — you'll be falling over yourself to make another jump.

BET YOU NEVER KNEW!

If you don't happen to have a parachute things can get a teensy bit more difficult. In 1944 Flight-Sergeant Nicholas Alkemade was in desperate danger 5,500 metres above Germany. His plane was on fire and his parachute was burnt to a cinder. He jumped and fully expected to die. But he was lucky. He fell on top of a tree and then onto a deep bank of snow and as a result much of the force of his fall was soaked up. Alkemade survived to tell his remarkable story and he didn't even break any bones!

MORE GRUESOME GRAVITY

In the past, gravity was used to make executions more efficient. During a hanging the victim dropped through a trapdoor and gravity acting on the rope broke the victim's neck. If the drop was too far, the force yanked their head off too. Gruesome!

Another gruesome method of execution was the guillotine. This featured a 30.4-kg weight attached to a sharp blade. The force powering the gruesome blade as it fell was gravity. In the 1790s working model guillotines were popular children's toys. Their parents must have been off their heads.

POOR TEDDY!

In England in the seventeenth century, criminals who refused to plead guilty or not guilty at their trials were crushed to death under heavy weights. Once again it was gravity doing the damage. You may be interested to know that a louse can withstand a force of 500,000 times its own weight. Unfortunately for the criminals, humans scrunch more easily.

Now for something a bit less fatal. Hopefully. You'd think that lying on a bed of nails would turn you into a gruesome human pin cushion. Surely gravity pins you to those nasty nails? Not necessarily. You can press down with a force of 450 g on a nail without harm. (Don't try proving this at home – nails are usually crawling with disgusting germs.) So 400 nails can support a huge 182 kg man for a comfortable night's sleep. Bet that's a weight off your mind.

FATAL EXPRESSIONS

ARGH! SLUGS! MY MASS HAS INCREASED!

SHOULD YOU GET HIM SOME SLUG KILLER?

ANSWER

No. He's got a weight problem. Scientists say "mass" instead of weight because weight is just a measure of how strongly gravity is pulling you towards the Earth. Also some scientists measure mass in a unit called the "slug". The overweight scientist in the picture weighs ten slugs (320 lbs). He should cut out chocolate and sticky puddings, or move to the moon. The moon's gravity is weaker than Earth's, so a human only weighs 1/6 as much there.

TEST YOUR TEACHER

Your teacher's bound to fall down on this really tricky question. Smile sweetly and say:

EXCUSE ME, IS IT TRUE THAT GRAVITY CAN HELP YOU LOSE WEIGHT?

ANSWER

Yes – but you'd have to be in a lift with a set of scales to prove it. If one day the lift cable snaps, quickly leap on the scales. In the few seconds you take to hurtle to the ground you're weightless! Weight is just a measure of gravity's pull. But when you fall you're not resisting gravity and you're weightless! You can blame Galileo for all this, he was the first person to discover how the force works.

Hall of fame: Galileo Galilei (1564–1642)
Nationality: Italian

Young Galileo wanted to study maths (strange boy), but his dad forced him to learn medicine instead. Doctors got more pay than mathematicians. But sneaky Galileo secretly studied sums until his dad gave up on him. When he was 25, Galileo became a maths professor at Pisa University. Then he got interested in gravity and performed amazing experiments to measure the force. Here's what his notebooks may have looked like.

GALILEO's BOOK of EXPERIMENTS

People laugh at me when I say that light and heavy things fall at the same speed. They say "Of course heavy things fall quicker - 'cos they're heavier." Grrr! I'll show them.

WOOD→ ○ ○ ←METAL

Experiment 1

1 Climb leaning Tower of Pisa with two balls of the same size. One ball is wooden and one is metal. Make sure the metal one is much heavier.

2 Reach top of tower. It's really slippery and there's no hand-rail. Careful now!

3 Chuck the two balls off the tower. Try not to chuck self off at same time.

4 Oh-nearly forgot. Check no one's underneath.

5 Note how balls land. If I'm right they'll both land at the same time.

MIAOW!

ME

People still don't believe me. Huh - this'll teach them a lesson.

Experiment 2

1 Get a wooden board with a little wooden gully on it. Line it with some nice shiny parchment made from animal skin with the fat scraped off.

USE SKIN FROM CAT KILLED IN EXPERIMENT 1

2 Raise the gully on a slope and roll a bronze ball down it. (If you don't have a bronze ball any other metal will do.)

3 Be sure to precisely measure the time taken for the ball to roll to the bottom of the slope. OOPS - silly me, I was about to forget, no one's invented an accurate clock yet. Better use pulse to time ball's speed. Mustn't get too excited, or my pulse will be racing. Better repeat the test a few times to make sure.

3, 4, 5, 6, 7. . .

RUMBLE RUMBLE

4 I believe gravity makes things accelerate at the same speed. If I'm right, balls of different weights will roll at the same speed too.

Notes:

1 Galileo was proved right in both experiments.

2 It should be pointed out that boring old historians reckon there's no proof Galileo performed the first experiment. Huh – why spoil a good story?

GALILEO'S GENIUS

There's no doubt Galileo was a genius. He invented the thermometer, a pendulum-driven clock and an amazing compass that you could use to work out the purity of metals. He even discovered that cannonballs fall in a curved path. They move forwards at a constant speed and downwards at an increasing speed under the influence of gravity. This fatal discovery helped gunners fire more accurately and kill more people.

Talking about killing people, Galileo nearly met a fiery fate. He used a telescope to prove that the Earth goes around the Sun. But the Church didn't agree. Galileo was put on trial and faced with a cruel choice: admit he was wrong or get tortured on the rack and burned to death. So what would you do? Tell a lie to stay alive or tell the truth and get cooked? Galileo told the judges he was wrong, even though he knew he was right. He was locked up at home for the rest of his life.

WOBBLY BALANCE

Everything has a centre of gravity. Imagine a tightrope walker.

Her centre of balance is the point inside her body where gravity is pulling most strongly. If this crucial point is supported underneath and the performer's weight is evenly balanced around it she's OK. If not there'll be a gloopy mess on the pavement. Yet some balancing acts seem impossible.

WOBBLY BALANCING QUIZ

See if you can guess which of these incredible balancing acts are true and which are false.

1 In 1553 a Dutch acrobat balanced on one foot on the weathervane of St Paul's Cathedral, London, waving a 4.6-metre streamer. And he didn't fall off. TRUE/FALSE

WHY ISN'T ANYONE ELSE WATCHING?

THEY'RE ALL INSIDE PRAYING HE DOESN'T FALL OFF

2 In 1859 French tightrope walker Jean Blondin (1824—1897) walked across the raging Niagara Falls 50 metres in the air. And he was wearing a blindfold. TRUE/FALSE

3 In 1773 Dutch acrobat Leopold van Trump juggled ten tomatoes whilst balancing on a tightrope 30 metres in the air. If he had fallen he might have invented tomato ketchup. TRUE/FALSE

4 In 1842 a Miss Cooke wowed London circus goers when she sat at a table and drank a glass of wine. Boring? Not really. Everything was balanced on a high wire. TRUE/FALSE

5 In 1995 Aleksandr Bendikov of Belarus balanced a pyramid made of 880 coins. The coin pyramid was upside down and balanced on top of the edge of a single coin. Luckily, no one needed change for the bus. TRUE/FALSE

6 In 1996 American Bryan Berg built a house of cards 100 storeys high – that's 5.85 metres. TRUE/FALSE

7 In 1990 Brazilian Leandro Henrique Basseto cycled on one wheel of his bicycle for 100 minutes. TRUE/FALSE

Yes, it's amazing what incredible death-defying, gravity-defying, balancing acts people can do just as long as the force of gravity is exactly balanced. But getting it right on the high-wire certainly puts you under pressure. And oddly enough, the next chapter is about pressure too. The kind of pressure that can fatally crush a human being. Ouch!

UNDER PRESSURE

Air and water are common enough on Earth but they contain vital chemicals – in fact we couldn't live without them. But if they're under pressure it's hard to live with them. And they can easily prove fatal.

Fatal forces fact file

Name:	Air and water pressure
The basic facts:	When tiny bits of air and water (molecules) are pushed aside by an object they push back. That's why when you get in a deep bath you can feel the water pushing against your body. It's what is called water pressure.
The horrible details:	The deeper you go, the more water there is above you. This means more pressure. Divers breathe air that's also under pressure to stop their lungs getting squashed.

One of the first people to study air pressure was French physicist Blaise Pascal.

Hall of fame: Blaise Pascal (1623–1662)
Nationality: French

Blaise Pascal had no sense of humour. Not surprising really, he suffered all his life from violent indigestion so he didn't have the stomach for too many jokes. But that didn't stop brainy Blaise from making some amazing discoveries. At the age of 19 he built a machine to help his tax collector dad count up the loot. And in 1646 he invented a barometer – a machine that measures air pressure. High air pressure pushes a column of mercury upwards.

To test his invention Blaise forced his brother-in-law to walk up a local mountain carrying the barometer. (The scientist's health wasn't up to making the climb himself, of course.) The climber found that the air pressure dropped as he went higher. The higher you go, the less air there is pushing down on you. Today the brave brother-in-law is forgotten but pressure is measured in "Pascals". (1 Pascal = 1 Newton per square metre.)

BET YOU NEVER KNEW!

Imagine all those kilometres of air above you pressing down on your head. The air pressure on your body is an incredible 100,000 Pascals. That's the same weight as two elephants. Luckily, the air inside your body is under pressure too. It pushes outwards with the same force so you don't even notice it. Planes that fly at high altitudes have pressurized cabins in which the air is kept at the same pressure as ground level. If a pilot flew without this protection, the lower air pressure would cause air bubbles in his or her body to get bigger. The guts and lungs would swell painfully and air bubbles trapped in fillings could make their teeth explode.

DARE YOU DISCOVER ... HOW AIR PRESSURE HELPS YOU DRINK?

You will need:

• Yourself • A bottle of your favourite drink (it's all in the interests of science) – just so long as the bottle's got a narrow neck.

What you do:

1 Try drinking from the bottle. Sit upright and tip the bottle up so it's level with your mouth. You can easily suck the liquid up.

2 Now stick the mouth of the bottle in your mouth. Wrap your lips around the neck of the bottle. Now try to drink.

What do you notice?

a) It's as easy as before.

b) You can't suck any more drink up.

c) You dribble uncontrollably into your drink.

b) Liquids flow to areas where the air pressure is less. As you try to suck your drink, the air space in the bottle gets bigger. Since no more air gets into the bottle, the air pressure drops below the air pressure in your mouth. This keeps the liquid in the bottle. Don't suck too hard – you might swallow the bottle. Mind you, that's not as horrible as a vacuum in your bottle. Here's why…

BET YOU NEVER KNEW!

A vacuum is a completely empty space where there's no air or water pressure. That means that if you absent-mindedly forgot your space suit when you went for a space walk, the air pressure in your lungs could burst them – with fatal results. Mind you, the lack of air would be just as fatal!

UNDER PRESSURE

1 The first man-made vacuum was made by Otto von Guericke (1602–1686) Mayor of Magdeburg, Germany. In his spare time Otto was keen on scientific experiments but in 1631 Magdeburg was destroyed in war and 70,000 people were killed. Von Guericke got away and carried on researching.

2 In 1647 he tried pumping air from a beer cask. But more air got in and made a strange whistling noise.

3 So he put the cask in a barrel of water. Water was sucked into the cask with a strange squelching noise.

4 Next he made a hollow copper ball. But when he pumped the air out it was crushed by an unseen force.

5 In 1654 von Guericke made a hollow ball from two stronger copper cups and pumped out the air. He'd made a vacuum. The pressure of the air outside jammed the cups together. It was this pressure that had crushed the earlier ball.

6 Fifty men couldn't pull the cups apart.

7 Two teams of horses didn't stand a chance.

8 But when von Guericke pumped air into the hollow centre the cups fell apart.

SOME PRESSING FACTS

1 In the 1890s Aimée, a young circus performer, used the power of vacuums to walk upside down. Her shoes had suction caps attached to them and as she walked the air was pushed out of the caps. The pressure of the air outside the caps then glued her feet to a board hung from the ceiling. Very im-press-ive!

2 Champagne in a bottle is under pressure too. This is due to all the gas bubbles squeezed into the drink.

When shaken and heated, the cork fires out at 12.3 metres a second – as fast as a rock blasted with dynamite. It definitely makes a party go with a bang.

3 Pressurized liquid or gases are used in hydraulic machines such as the powerful pistons that lift crane jibs. One early hydraulic machine was a nineteenth-century vacuum cleaner. Water was squirted one way and the falling pressure sucked in air and dirt behind it. But when water went the wrong way it flooded your home.

4 In 1868 American inventor George Westinghouse (1846–1914) made an air brake. It used the cushioning effect of air pressure to halt a train. Rail tycoon Cornelius Vanderbilt called it a "foolish notion". He didn't think air could stop a train. But nowadays air brakes are used on buses and lorries too.

Air pressure can do amazing things but could it also haul a train? It took a genius to see the possibilities in this "train of thought". A hard-driving ruthless workaholic genius in a black top hat.

Hall of fame: Isambard Kingdom Brunel (1806–1859) **Nationality:** British

Isambard Kingdom Brunel dedicated his life to engineering. He developed some spectacular engineering projects that used the forces of nature to help make people's lives easier. He built railways, giant iron ships, bridges and tunnels on a grand scale. At times he was so wrapped up in his work that he showed little concern for others. He even sent his crippled son to a school where there were daily floggings. When the child complained, bossy Brunel snapped at him: "It is very distressing, but one must put up with it."

Issie loved to attempt the seemingly impossible. Sometimes he was successful, but he also made many fatal mistakes. This story is about one of them … a railway powered by air pressure.

PIPE DREAMS

Devon, England 1848

Isambard Kingdom Brunel chewed on his giant-sized cigar as he strode angrily along the railway. As usual his mind was jumping with ideas. Fantastic ideas. Mighty plans. Pipe dreams. They had all seemed so easy. Once.

Four years ago Brunel and some other leading engineers visited Ireland to see the world's first "atmospheric railway". A railway where the carriages were pulled quickly and silently. Pulled along by the amazing power of air.

The idea was simple...

How to build your own atmospheric railway.

CROSS-SECTION OF PIPE

LEATHER HINGE

PISTON ATTACHED TO UNDERSIDE OF TRAIN

LEATHER HINGE FITS OVER SLOT

IRON TUBE WITH SLOT

PISTON FITS INSIDE IRON TUBE

And here's how it worked.

1 Powerful steam engines pump the air from the pipe.
2 A piston travels along the pipe. It's pushed by air trying to rush back into the vacuum.
3 The piston is linked to passenger carriages and provides the moving power.

The other engineers laughed at the strangely silent railway. They thought it was impractical. But Isambard was quietly impressed. He suggested using atmospheric pressure for the South Devon Railway. But he forgot to mention to anyone that the Irish railway was always breaking down. Little old ladies rushed to sink their savings in a scheme backed by the world's greatest engineer. But the pipe dream soon turned into a pipe nightmare.

Now Brunel had come to see things for himself and young Tom the signalman's boy was showing him around.

"It's the leather hinges, Mr Brunel," said Tom slightly in awe of the great man. "They dry and crack in cold winter weather. And they rot in warm sunshine."

"So I see," said Brunel wrinkling his nose in distaste. "What's that appalling smell?"

"That'll be the fish oil. The railway pays people to walk along the line and paint the leather with soap and fish liver oil to keep it soft. Smells disgusting, it does."

They walked on until they reached one of the massive brick-built pumping sheds.

"Here's the other problem!" cried Tom. He nervously twisted his pale sweaty fingers. "It's the pipes…"

"What do you mean pipes?" bellowed Brunel above the noise of the engines. The huge steam engine snorted foul black smoke like an angry dragon. The gasping pumps sucked the air from the hollow iron pipes. And with the air came a stream of horrible things.

Oily water, rust and dead rats.

Rats. *Water.*

"How did they get there?" Brunel roared into the boy's ear. But he'd already guessed the terrible truth.

Hungry rats chewed the oily leather flaps until they were no longer air-tight. Water seeped in and rusted the pipes.

The famous engineer strode on furiously with the signalman's boy jogging to keep up. Suddenly Brunel bent down to touch the rat-nibbled leather. Tom watched in fascinated horror. "No!" he shouted.

Brunel had his hand on the flap when Tom grabbed his arm.

"Stand aside boy!" ordered Brunel curtly.

"*Please* don't touch it," gasped Tom.

"Why NOT?"

Then Brunel saw the ghastly danger.

The vacuum inside the pipe wasn't 100 per cent. But it could still pluck his finger bones from their sockets. Scrunch, squelch, plop. No more fingers.

He backed off, muttering. There were some things even the great Brunel dared not do.

In February 1848 Brunel told the Company the problems were almost solved. But seven months later he advised the directors to scrap the entire project. The little old ladies had lost their savings. And they were angry.

So how did Brunel make it up to them?

a) He offered to build a new railway for nothing.

b) He said he wouldn't send his bill for engineering advice.

c) He offered them a lifetime's supply of smelly fish oil.

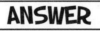
ANSWER

b) Brunel kindly offered not to send his bill. Not just yet. Bet that cheered them up. There was a lot of anger and friction. You get friction in the world of forces too. But this sort of friction can wreck machines and spark fatal fires. That's why the next chapter is *RED HOT.*

FACTS ABOUT FRICTION

Newton said that a moving object would carry on moving for ever if another force didn't slow it down. That force is called friction. People use the word friction to mean aggro, anger or annoyance. Like a really bad day at school. And in the world of fatal forces, friction can also often spoil your whole day.

Fatal forces fact file

Name: Friction

The basic facts: You get friction when two moving objects brush together. Tiny bumps on each side stick together. They make heat and sound as the energy of moving objects turns into heat and sound energy.

The horrible details: Friction causes problems for machines because it slows them down or makes them overheat. But lack of friction also causes fatal problems. If your bike brake blocks get worn they can't grip the wheels with enough friction. So you can't stop. Help!

Mind you, the man who discovered friction had an amazing life story. He could almost have been a character from friction — er, fiction.

Hall of fame: Benjamin Thompson
(Count Rumford of Bavaria) (1753–1814)
Nationality: American

Ben Thompson was a teacher who escaped from school. He was born in the United States and besides being a teacher, he was a gymnast and a medical student. Until the war. The American colonists were fighting for their independence from Britain. But which side should Ben choose? The Americans or the British?

Rumour has it that he chose both. He spied for the British *and* the Americans. He was a sort of a double-agent. But the British never knew this and King George III gave Ben a knighthood when the war was over.

But Ben liked the excitement of being at war. He said he didn't want to "vegetate in England". So what did he do? Simple! He went to Bavaria as a special adviser on war to the government and became Minister for War in 1793.

As Minister of War, Ben devised a cunning plan. The streets were full of beggars and the army was short of uniforms. Ben's idea was to force the beggars to make uniforms. But how should he feed the beggars? After much research Ben found the cheapest food was watery vegetable soup. So he "vegetated" in Bavaria instead of in England – ha, ha. Ben was so keen on his idea he even published a book of recipes. Could this be a new line in school dinners? Then he had a second brainwave.

He put soldiers to work growing potatoes to make the soup to feed the beggars who made their uniforms. Ben's plan was a great success so at least it didn't land him in the soup! Brainy Ben made many other interesting discoveries. A new chimney for houses, a new stove and a coffee percolator to put on the stove.

And then he discovered friction.

One day Ben was watching a cannon being made. The barrel of the cannon was bored by a drill. Ben could feel the heat wafting off the cannon. In those days people thought heat was an invisible liquid. But Ben found you got extra heat if you used a blunt drill. So he figured the heat was produced by the drill. Dead right. The blunt drill had tiny bumps on its surface – and this caused extra friction. And more heat.

FACT OR FRICTION?

Often, just like Benjamin Thompson, physicists draw conclusions from things they notice. Could you do this? Here are some everyday happenings. Which ones are caused by friction?

1 Friction helps you to build a house of cards.
2 Friction explains how you can whip a tablecloth off a fully laid table without breaking anything.

3 Friction makes electrical equipment heat up.
4 The patterns on tyres cause friction with the road. This helps to control the vehicle.

5 People use friction to start fires.

6 Friction helps skiers to ski up hills.

WHO CARES ABOUT FRICTION! WHY CAN'T WE USE THE SKI-LIFT LIKE EVERYONE ELSE?

7 Runners use friction to run without slipping.

8 Friction causes people to get burnt by snow.

ANSWERS

1 Fact. Tiny bumps on the surface of the cards help them to stick to the surface of the table. That's friction. It works if the cards are at a steep angle.

2 Fiction. The inertia of the crockery and the force of gravity pins it to the table. If you pull the tablecloth fast enough there isn't enough friction to pull the crockery off the table. However, practising this trick at home may cause fatal friction with your family.

3 Fact. As the electrical current runs through the circuits it causes friction which heats up the machine. That's why TVs can burst into flames if you cover their ventilation holes.

4 Fiction. Smooth tyres provide more friction in dry weather. The treads are better in wet weather. The wheel scoops the water out of the way so the tyres can grip the road.

5 Fact. One of your ancestors hit on a hot method of lighting fires. Rub two sticks together. The heat of the friction can set fire to some dried fungus. Later on people found that partially burnt underwear caught fire again very easily. So it was ideal for getting a blaze going.

6 Fact. Traditional up-hill skis used sealskin for this purpose. Nowadays they have man-made bristles. It's kinder to seals.

7 Fact. Spiked shoes increase friction with the track.

8 Fact. Crazy skiers can suffer serious burns if they go too fast and then fall over. At high speeds, friction causes enough heat to burn the skin before the snow melts.

MESSED-UP MACHINES

Here's the bad news about friction. It slows machines down. Yes, it's a real spanner in the works for generations of freaky physicists who've tried to devise the ultimate machine. One that keeps on working without power. Perpetual motion.

Between 1617 and 1906 the British Patent Office received ideas for 600 perpetual motion machines. None worked.

Here are three more. Which one was successful?

1 A self-powered pump
The water-lifting pump is powered by a waterwheel that is powered by water falling from buckets tied to the wheel as it runs around.

2 A perpetual bicycle
The power for this bike comes from your bum bouncing on the saddle. This drives the rear wheel

using a drive belt. So you could cycle for ever or until you get a sore bum.

3 A perpetual wind machine
Dreamt up by an Italian doctor in 1500. Air from the fan is funnelled down a horn linked to a propeller which in turn powers the fan.

ANSWER

None of them! The fatal truth is that perpetual motion is as about as likely as a vegetarian vampire bat. Here's why…

A hot halt

Perpetual motion, unfortunately, breaks a law of physics. The Second Law of Thermodynamics to be exact. (Thermodynamics is the branch of physics to do with heat and energy. It's a subject you can really warm to.) The Second Law of Thermodynamics says that energy is lost from a machine as sound, noise, heat and, of course, friction.

So the machine stops because it runs out of energy. By the way, the First Law of Thermodynamics says you can turn energy from motion into heat. And it's true. Try rubbing your hands and friction turns the energy of your moving hands into a nice warm sensation.

A SLIPPERY SUBJECT

Sometimes we want friction. Brakes, tyres, rubber-soled shoes, sandpaper and driving belts in machines would be useless without it.

But sometimes we don't want friction. We want things to go smoothly. That's why some slippery character invented lubrication. A lubricant such as oil fills out the little bumps that cause friction and allows the surfaces to slide past one another.

Most winter sports depend on lubrication. Sledges, skis and skates move easily because they melt a thin layer of ice beneath them. So they float along on this watery lubricant without too much friction.

Until you slip over.

VERY LITTLE FRICTION

LOTS OF FRICTION

Lubrication also launches ships. That's why in the Middle Ages slipways were coated in revoltingly greasy animal fat. A slave got the risky job of knocking away the props under the ship. At the last minute the slave had to jump clear. If he slipped, the ship would crush him – that's why they called it the slip-way. If the slave survived he was given his freedom.

But if lubrication is lethal, friction can be fatal. That was certainly the case in Rome four centuries ago.

FATAL FRICTION

Rome, 1586

It was an ancient obelisk. For 2,000 years it had lain forgotten in the dirt, west of St Peter's Cathedral. But times had changed. The Pope decided that the stone would look great in front of St Peter's. But how could it be raised? It was quite a problem. The obelisk weighed 327 tonnes.

"They say," murmured old Roberto, "that two engineers turned down the job. Reckoned it couldn't be done."

"I can see why," replied young Marco gazing in awe at the huge stone in its protective cage.

"Well – we'd better give it a try. Gotta earn our pay," grumbled Roberto with a wheezy cough. He and Marco were amongst hundreds of sailors hired to raise the obelisk.

They took up their ropes.

The square was ringed by crowds. Thousands of people were cheering and waving handkerchiefs and waiting impatiently for the big event. A smartly dressed young man leapt onto a platform.

Roberto screwed up his creased old face in a scowl. "That's Fontana – he's the engineer who claims he can do it. What a big-head!"

"People of Rome!" proclaimed the young man. "Today we'll raise this great monument from the past. When the trumpet sounds, you sailors must pull the ropes. Only stop when you hear the bell. It's vital that these signals are obeyed in silence. There must be no talking on pain of death!" The young man pointed sternly to the nearby gallows.

There was a shocked silence.

The older sailor made the sign of the cross. "That's a bit over the top," he whispered.

The sailors spat on their hands. The moist spit would stop friction with the rope burning the skin off their fingers.

The trumpet blared. The harsh note echoed around the square. Silently the men took the strain. The ropes creaked. Windlasses squealed. Capstans groaned round. Slowly, painfully, the great stone began to lift.

Then the bell rang. Everyone rested for a few moments. The trumpet sounded again. Once again the sailors' muscles bunched and knotted until sweat trickled down their backs. Then disaster struck.

The ropes jammed – halted by friction between the ropes and windlasses. The sailors pulled the ropes until their faces screwed up in agony. Nothing moved. The taut ropes groaned and frayed. The stone tottered. Young Marco saw the danger. He shouted instantly: "Water, give water to the ropes!" Then he realized what he'd done. And knew he must die.

"Seize him!" screamed Fontana, his voice cracking with tension and disappointment. "Seize him for breaking the silence!"

Strong arms grabbed Marco. The guards dragged the young sailor towards the scaffold and the waiting executioner. The people gasped in horror but no one dared speak.

"I'm sorry," whispered Marco. But it was too late.

The executioner tightened the harsh hemp rope around Marco's bare throat.

A thin, old priest touched the sailor's arm.

"What's your last request?" the priest mumbled.

"Please, father," croaked Marco. His heart was racing and he couldn't speak clearly. His throat was dry and the rope didn't help. "Please, tell them to pour water on the ropes."

"I don't know if that's possible, my son."

"*Please* do it!"

The steel-helmeted guards beat their drums. It was the signal for the execution to begin.

The priest hurried over to Fontana. The young engineer nodded his head impatiently. A large water pitcher was found and its contents poured over the straining ropes.

"Come on mate, let's get it over with," said the executioner cheerfully shoving Marco up the ladder of death.

Just then a trumpet blared and the ropes took the strain.

"Why were the people cheering?" thought Marco wildly. Were they pleased to see him die?

No. The ropes were moving easily. The stone was being lifted smoothly and quickly. At the foot of the ladder stood Domenico Fontana. Shamefaced.

"Release that man!" he shouted.

As a sailor Marco was used to hauling wet ropes at sea. He knew that there was less friction on wet ropes because the water acted as a lubricant. You'll be pleased to know that the brave sailor was pardoned and given his freedom. But what was his reward for saving the obelisk?

a) A golden pitcher of water.

b) Tea with the Pope.

c) His very own ship.

ANSWER

b) He met the Pope as a VIP guest. And the sailor's home town of San Remo was given the honour of providing palms for the annual St Peter's Palm Sunday parade.

Well, hopefully you won't slip-up over this easy experiment.

DARE YOU DISCOVER ... HOW TO GIVE THINGS THE SLIP?

You will need:

BANANA

COOKING OIL

COOKING OIL

PLASTIC BOTTLE TOP

KITCHEN TOWELS

TWO PLASTIC FOOD TRAYS

What you do:

1 Flick the bottle top along the first tray. Make sure the top stays on the tray and doesn't fly through the air.

2 Carefully pour a few drops of cooking oil on the first tray. Smear it over the surface with a kitchen towel until the surface is shiny and there is no extra oil on the tray.

3 Now flick the bottle top again as hard as before. Note what happens.

4 Mash up the banana and, using another kitchen towel, smear a little of the mixture over the second tray. Make sure the surface is smooth and shiny and there are no lumps of banana left.

5 *(optional)* Mash the remaining banana with a little cream and sugar. Eat it. Tell your feeble-minded folks it's all part of the experiment. Who said science was tough?

6 Now flick the bottle top again as hard as before. *What do you notice?*

a) Both the oil and the banana make good lubricants. They help the top move faster.

b) The top stuck to the banana and skimmed along over the oil.

c) The top stuck in the oil but skimmed over the banana.

ANSWER

a) Lubricating oils are squeezed from peanuts, coconuts or bits of dead fish. In some countries bananas are used because they're slippery too. That's why you slip on a banana skin!

HORRIBLE HEALTH WARNING!

Please do not test your lubricants in any of the following places:

1. School corridors – they're slippery enough already.

2. Your teacher's chair.

3. Stairs. They could prove your downfall!

PATIENCE BEING STRETCHED →

SCHOOL TIE BEING STRETCHED

Any of these things could stretch a grown-up's patience to breaking point. But you ain't seen nothing yet. The next chapter's really taking the strain.

STRETCHING AND STRAINING

Hold an elastic band between your fingers. Pull one end ever so carefully. The elastic band is storing the energy you put into pulling it. Let go – the released energy sends the elastic band flying. Oh dear – why does a teacher always get in the way? But just tell him that it's all part of a very technical scientific experiment – he'll understand! One of the first people to experiment with stretching was scientist Robert Hooke.

Hall of fame: Robert Hooke (1635–1703)
Nationality: British

After his bust-ups with Newton (see page 24), Robert must have known all about tension. But this talented scientist was interested in everything from telescopes to making flying machines that didn't fly. Incredibly, he also worked as an architect, an astronomer, a mechanic and a model maker. Yes. Hooke liked working at full-stretch.

According to one story, Robert wrote a strange code in his will which deciphered into Latin reads *"ut tensio sic vis"*. Mean anything to you? Thought not. Further translated into English it means "as the extension so the force". And these weird words turned out to be Hooke's Law on stretching. Imagine hanging a weight on a spring – the spring stretches. Double the weight and the spring stretches twice as far. Simple, innit?

DARE YOU DISCOVER 1 ... WHAT HAPPENS WHEN SOMETHING STRETCHES?

You will need:

• Yourself • A 0.5-cm-thick elastic band

What you do:

1 Suddenly stretch the elastic band.

2 Put it against your face.

What happens and why?

a) The elastic band feels strangely cold because all the energy has been stretched out of it.

b) The elastic band feels warm. This is due to the energy that you have provided by stretching it.

c) The elastic band feels warm because stretching causes friction with your hot sweaty little fingers.

ANSWER

b) The band briefly stores energy from the force that stretches it. The energy tries to escape as heat and that's why the band feels hot.

DARE YOU DISCOVER 2 ... THE POWER OF AN ELASTIC BAND?

Here's a machine that uses stored energy in an elastic band to get moving. Ask an adult to help with some of the cutting.

You will need:

SCISSORS

PARCEL TAPE

MATCHSTICK WITH HEAD CUT OFF

CANDLE

COTTON REEL

PENCIL

ELASTIC BAND

What you do:

1 Cut 2.5 cm off the bottom of the candle.

2 Remove the wick from the wax and make its middle hole large enough for the elastic band.

3 Pass the elastic band through the centres of the candle stump and the cotton reel.

4 Pass the matchstick through the elastic band at its cotton reel end. Secure the matchstick with a strip of parcel tape.

5 Pass the pencil through the elastic band at its candle end.

6 Wind the elastic band by turning the pencil. Watch your vehicle creep along as the elastic band unwinds. Compare its performance on rough and smooth slopes.

What do you notice?

a) It climbs better on smooth slopes.

b) It climbs better on rough slopes.

c) It can't climb slopes.

ANSWER

b) The machine uses the force you put into turning the elastic band to move. The friction provided by rough slopes helps your machine grip the ground and climb better.

A STRETCHY SUBJECT

Here's some more elastic info to stretch your brain cells. A few hundred years ago you could be sent to prison in England for a long stretch. Stretched out on a timber frame with rollers at each end. This was the rack. The most anyone was ever stretched on a rack was 15 cm. After that their arm and leg joints popped out of their sockets. Rumours that racks were used in schools are just "tall stories". No – teachers just racked children's *brains*.

In the 1700s rubber thread was used in clothes and underwear. Sadly, the rubber melted in hot weather and cracked in cold.

In 1839 scientists discovered a chemical treatment that stopped this happening and rubber thread known as elastic was used in corsets and knickers from the 1930s. (Corsets are the tight-fitting garments some women wore to squeeze their bulging bodies into shape. Before elastic, corsets were reinforced with bits of whale bone.)

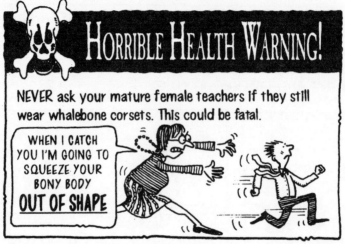

HORRIBLE HEALTH WARNING!

NEVER ask your mature female teachers if they still wear whalebone corsets. This could be fatal.

WHEN I CATCH YOU I'M GOING TO SQUEEZE YOUR BONY BODY **OUT OF SHAPE**

Nowadays man-made elastic is used for much more than just corsets – including the rope bungee jumpers use. Would you want to bungee jump?

If your answer to this question is "ARGGGGGH!" you wouldn't envy Gregory Riffi who in 1992 jumped 249.9 metres from a helicopter over France.

With his life hanging by a thread – all right – an elastic rope.

By the way, bungee jumping isn't usually fatal if it's done by experts. But as the jumper falls, the blood rushes to their head and this can make their eyeballs bleed a bit. Another sport that depends on stretching is archery.

BIG BAD BOWS

1 The bow was invented before 20,000 BC. The idea was that you could store energy by pulling back the string and transfer the force of the energy to fire the arrow.

2 Five seconds later the bow may have claimed its first victim. Ooops!

3 In ancient times someone in central Asia hit upon a better bow. It was made from grisly bits of animal horn and tendons and strengthened with wood. The outward curve of the bow allowed it to be drawn with greater force.

4 Meanwhile the ancient Greeks and Chinese were using crossbows. This deadly weapon could fire a bolt 305 metres.

5 But the crossbow string had to be cranked slowly back. And during that time ordinary archers with ordinary bows were so skilled, they could turn the crossbow soldier into a pin-cushion in no time – unless he bolted first.

6 And then a Welsh person invented the long-bow. It could fire an arrow 320 metres. And straight through chain mail. At shorter ranges, the arrows could pierce armour too.

7 Modern bows are really high-tech.

SIGHT

TOUGH CARBON
AND FIBRE
STRIPS
GLUED
TOGETHER

GRIP

PHOTO OF
TEACHER
FOR TARGET
PRACTICE

NICE STRONG
ARTIFICIAL
FIBRE STRING

8 In free-style shooting, the archers lie on their back, strap the bow to their feet and draw the string with both hands. Of course, it isn't only stretchy things that can store force. Springs can do this too when you push them down and then they pop up again. You'll be surprised to know that the earliest springs were used 600 years ago in mousetraps. And springs can spring real surprises on you. Here are seven more.

SEVEN SPRINGY SURPRISES

1 The first toasters sold in 1919 had powerful springs that shot toast into the air. Bet that surprised a few people.

2 Springs sometimes break. Metal fatigue does for a cheap spring after about 100,000 extensions, but a better spring lasts over 10,000,000 extensions. A surprisingly long stretch.

3 Bed springs are a surprising shape. They're cone shaped – that's wider at their top than at the base. This makes them squeeze easily at first but the harder they're pressed the more difficult they are to squash. A bed that feels comfy and springy to you feels like a rock to a big, sprawling grown-up.

4 You know the circus act where a person is fired from a cannon? You may be surprised to discover that springs, rather than explosions, are used to provide the necessary force. The bang was a firework let off to make it look like the cannon had really fired.

5 And did you know we've got springs in our legs too? The ligaments that hold your joints together are a bit springy and your S-shaped backbone jogs up and down as you walk. Together they'll put a spring in your step.

6 In the 1970s two American scientists trained a pair of kangaroos to hop on a treadmill. The scientists found that kangaroos jump using their springy tendons. It's a bit like jumping on a pogo stick.

7 Springy things are important for sport. Traditional

tennis rackets were very expensive and strung with springy sheep's guts. Sounds like a bit of a racket. And talking about springy sports equipment, trainers have to be springy too.

SUPER SPRINGY SHOES

Do this to your brother's trainers and you'd better run for it before he takes a swing at you. Funnily enough the next chapter's about swinging and spinning too. Better stand clear.

GETTING IN A SPIN

Ever wondered why cars don't have square wheels? No – me neither. Well – round wheels go round better (howls of amazement). Also the force on the outer parts of the wheel produces greater force at the axle. And this is ideal for wheel-based machines such as waterwheels and cars. And there's lots more wheel-life facts to go around (and pathetic jokes too)…

Fatal forces expressions

STOP IT! IT'S CONSERVATION OF ANGULAR MOMENTUM!

Who's to blame?

No one – his 10p is rolling away. He's describing how coins and any other spinning objects have a habit of turning until another force gets in the way. That's why wheels work so well. Best put your foot over the coin and pretend you haven't seen it.

And wheels are wonderful. They were invented by some bright spark who lived in the Middle East in about 3500 BC. When a wheel goes around, centripetal force tries to pull it towards its centre – remember that force from page 38? And now let's face a few more facts to get your head spinning ... Oh go on – give it a whirl!

Fatal forces fact file

Name:

The basic facts:

Centripetal force

Imagine whirling a small ball around your head on a bit of string.

1 Centripetal force tries to move the ball towards the centre of its spin.

2 When you let go, the ball's momentum sends it flying off at an angle in a straight line.

The horrible details: A bolas uses centripetal force for catching animals or people. It's two balls on a rope. You whirl the bolas above your head and let go. The rope winds around your target's legs. Here's how to make your own.

HANG ON WHAT DID YOU SAY ABOUT CENTRIPETAL FORCE?

If centripetal force is making you dizzy, this rhyme might help you...

Centripetals in a spin
All the time it's pulling in
Let go the string – it's worth a try
In a straight line it will fly

DARE YOU DISCOVER ... HOW A BOLAS WORKS?

You will need:

• Two balls of Blu-Tack each 2.5 cm across

• A piece of strong string or twine 52 cm long

What you do:

1 Wrap a ball of Blu-Tack around each end of the string.

2 Squeeze the Blu-Tack to make sure it is holding the string securely.

3 Now you can practise throwing it. Hold the string between your thumb and fingers half-way between the two balls. Whirl the string round your head. Let go.

WHIZzzz

NOTE: READ HEALTH WARNING FIRST

1 Practising throwing your bolas indoors could be fatal for you if it knocks any priceless ornaments off the mantelpiece. Much better to practise outside in a wide open space.

2 Try to resist the temptation to throw your bolas at a small brother/sister/cat/dog, even if it is in the interest of science. You could use a small tree for target practice instead.

From your observations how does the bolas work?

a) Centripetal force makes the bolas fly straight. When the force stops it wraps round the tree trunk.

b) The bolas flies straight until centripetal force does the wrapping.

c) Centripetal force makes the bolas come back like a boomerang.

b) When you release the string, the momentum of the bolas makes it fly off in a straight line in the direction it was heading when you let go. When it hits the tree, centripetal force on the string wraps the bolus around the trunk.

GOING ROUND IN CIRCLES

Between them, centripetal force and momentum keep the show on the road and ensure that wheels are an all-round success story. They're useful for cars and trains, and buses and bikes, and tractors and windmills, and capstans that raise anchors. And thousands of other things too. Here are some amazing uses for wheels.

Weird wheels

1 The big Ferris wheels you see in funfairs were first invented in Russia in the 1600s. They were said to be inspired by the custom of giving children rides in the wheels used to scoop water from rivers. If the wheels went round too fast the children would be thrown into the river.

2 The name actually comes from American showman George Ferris who built a 75-metre wheel in 1893. Trouble is it took 20 minutes to go round once. Sounds as thrilling as watching porridge cool.

3 Wacky inventor Joseph Merlin gate-crashed a London party to show off the roller skates he'd just invented. The eighteenth-century boffin glided along playing his violin and feeling dead cool as he swished across the polished floor. Until he found he couldn't stop and crashed into a mirror. Merlin's problem was that his wheels spun easily on the smooth floor. And there wasn't much friction to slow them down. Bet he was really cut up about it.

4 By turning a wheel you can produce a force that can be used to power all kinds of machines. In the nineteenth century prisoners were put on the treadmill. They had to climb a revolting revolving wheel but they never reached the top because the wheel kept turning towards them. In the rotting prison ships the treadmills operated the pumps that stopped the ship sinking!

IT'S THE HAMSTER FOOD THAT REALLY GETS ME DOWN

BET YOU NEVER KNEW!
Remember the imaginary force from page 38? As the scientist cycled round the corner she felt as if a force was trying to throw her outwards. Some people wrongly think this is a real force called "centrifugal force". They imagine the force making a lasso fly through the air in a cowboy movie. Well, sorry folks – it doesn't really exist!

TEST YOUR TEACHER

The non-existent force is caused by an object's inertia, which opposes centripetal force. So can your teacher tell the difference between this effect a) and b) centripetal force? Or will their head start spinning instead?

1 It's used in labs to separate red blood cells from the rest of the blood.

2 The reason a pendulum swings more slowly in Central Africa than in Europe. (This is true.)

3 It helps your bike go round a corner.

4 The reason that you can whizz upside down on a roller-coaster and not fall out even if you weren't strapped in.

5 The reason why a spacecraft doesn't fall to Earth.

6 You'll find this inside a rotor. That's the theme park ride that whirls you around as the floor drops away leaving you stuck to the wall.

ANSWERS

1a The machine is called a centrifuge. It consists of a wheel on which a container is secured. The wheel whirls round hundreds of times a minute and the heavier cells in the blood sink to the bottom. A centrifuge is also used to separate the lighter cream from the rest of the milk. And they don't use the same machine!

2a There's a special bonus point if your teacher can explain how it works. As the Earth spins round, its middle – otherwise known as the equator – bulges slightly. This is why gravity is a bit weaker than at the Poles – and weaker gravity explains the pendulum puzzle. Our old pal Newton suggested this answer. In 1735, French expeditions to Peru and Lapland proved that our planet really is bulging.

3b But you remembered that from page 130 – didn't you? In fact the centripetal force is supplied by friction between your tyres and the road.

4a But it only works as long as you keep moving. Stop and you'll fall out – which is why it's essential to be strapped in.

5a Imagine you're flying round the Earth. The surface curves away beneath you. This increase in distance cancels out the effects of gravity as you fall. If you weren't moving so fast you would fall to Earth with fatal results!

6b You spin so fast that you stick to the wall. And if you vomit, your sick sticks to you.

TEACHER'S TEA-BREAK TEASER
If you are feeling madly brave, knock on the staffroom door. When it groans, creaks, or scrapes open, smile sweetly at your teacher and say:

EXCUSE ME, I WAS WONDERING WHY WHEN YOU STIR YOUR TEA, THE TEA LEAVES SETTLE AT THE CENTRE OF THE BOTTOM OF YOUR TEA CUP? SURELY THE TEA LEAVES SHOULD MOVE TOWARDS THE SIDES OF THE CUP?

ANSWER

Incredibly two of the world's greatest scientists puzzled over this for years. That's Nobel Prize winners Albert Einstein (1879-1955) and Erwin Schrödinger (1887-1961). In 1926 Mrs S asked Erwin the question but he didn't know the answer. So she asked Einstein. After many calculations Einstein worked out the answer and even wrote an article about it in 1933.

According to Einstein, momentum does move the tea leaves towards the sides of the cup. But friction between the liquid and the sides slows down the tea leaves at the sides and base of the cup. As the liquid stops turning the leaves fall towards the centre of the cup. Wow! And you thought it was just a cup of tea! Here's another amazing story to keep things swinging.

GETTING IN THE SWING

It was 1586 and 17-year-old Galileo (yes, him again) was in Pisa Cathedral listening to a boring sermon. He noticed a chandelier swinging in the breeze. Sometimes it swung in a long arc and sometimes in a shorter swing. But each swing seemed to take the same time.

So Galileo timed the swings using his pulse. He was right. (Could you make a similar discovery during a boring science lesson?)

Galileo used this newly discovered fact to design a new kind of clock. The grandfather clock used a swinging pendulum to keep time. What a time-ly invention.

In 1650 two priests spent a whole day counting the swings of a pendulum in a bid to prove the pendulum really did keep time. It did and they counted 87,998 swings.

87,941
WAKE
87,942
UP
87,943
FATHER!

But one sickly scientist had even bigger pendulum plans.

Hall of fame: Jean Bernard Léon Foucault

(1819–1868) **Nationality:** French

Young Jean was a sickly child. And his parents reckoned school would finish him off, so they educated him at home. Why can't all parents be so considerate? Poor Jean was never any good at his lessons. For a time he went nowhere. His bid to become a surgeon failed after he ran away from an operation. One squirt of blood and a bit of suffering and wimpy Jean burst into tears.

But Jean loved writing. So he became a science journalist instead. Then he got interested in experiments. He measured the speed of light and tried to photograph the stars. He then became fascinated by the idea that you could use a pendulum to prove the Earth turned during the day. Although everyone knew this, no one had ever tried to prove it actually happened.

In 1851 Jean devised an amazing test. He hung a huge steel ball 60 cm in diameter and weighing 30.4 kg from the dome of the Pántheon in Paris, a large building where many famous people were buried.

The illustration shows columns with a pendulum, and labels: PENDULUM, SPIKE, NERVOUS SCIENTIST, SAND.

The night before...

Last minute preparations for the big day. A brave worker climbs a very high ladder to check the cable is secured to the roof. The pendulum itself is tied to the wall by a cord. At last everything is ready!

NOTES We can't have the pendulum swinging around until the experiment is ready to start.

Later that night...

nibble! chew!

I can't sleep for nerves. I've been working to set up this experiment for months. Had to get the permission from Emperor Napoleon III himself. Will everything work?

The press are going to be there too. If this experiment fails I'll be the laughing stock of all France. Gulp!

Press

Sand

Up early - groan! Last minute preparations. Sprinkle floor with sand. Talk to reporters, say everything will be fine. Oh dear, I hope I'm right. Supposing the pendulum stops swinging...

Mid-morning...

Blimey! Look at all those people. All come to see my experiment. Better make a little speech. Then I'll set fire to the cord holding back the pendulum. My fingers shake. Ouch - I've burnt them. Hope it's not a bad omen.

NOTES If you simply push the pendulum it might not swing straight.

Lunch-time...

NOTES This track should get wider. The pendulum's swing shouldn't alter but as the ground turns underneath, the track will seem to move to the side. That's the idea anyway.

track

I can't take my eyes off the pendulum. It swings quite slowly and the spike makes a track in the sand on the floor.

145

Still swinging. Time seems to drag. I count the swings. It's like counting sheep.
I'm dozing off. Yawn - should have got more sleep last night. Zzzzzzzzzz z z

An hour later ...

Still swinging. Nothing happening. I should have known this right from the start. Maybe I could push the pendulum to one side when no one's looking. Help! The Emperor's glaring at me and he's really cross. I'M FINISHED. PANIC STATIONS!!!!

Nap III glaring

← Still sleeping

Just then . . .
I open my eyes. Phew! It must have been a dream. Everyone's pointing to the sand and talking. THE TRACK HAS GOT WIDER. I'M SAVED!!!

The world really does go round. YIPPEEEEE! I feel like dancing about and kissing everyone.

146

Foucault found himself a hero. He was awarded the *Légion d'Honneur* medal. He went on to invent gyroscopes which work on the same principle as spinning tops as you'll see in a moment. And tops are top toys for freaky physicists.

TOP TRICKS

Physicists like nothing better than playing with their favourite toys. Well, according to them they're investigating forces. Oh, yeah.

There are loads of toys that use the forces of spinning. Toys like yo-yos, hula-hoops, frisbees. And tops. A top was a favourite toy of Nobel prize winner Wolfgang Pauli (1900–1958) who was trying to work out the physics of inertia. Here's some crucial info to get *you* "tops" of the class.

Tops balance because angular momentum keeps them going – remember the coin running away from the scientist? Tops keep turning in the same way despite the efforts of gravity to pull them down. Bigger tops need more effort to get going but spin for longer. Tops are popular with kids the world over. Here's a traditional Inuit game you might like to play when it gets really cold.

You will need:

IGLOO

SPINNING TOP

What you do:

Spin the top. Run round your igloo (or house). Try to get back inside before the top falls down. (This could be fatal if you don't wrap up warm first.)

In 1743 English inventor John Smeaton (1724–1792) invented a sort of top that would stay level even on a ship in a storm. This allowed mariners to check where the horizon should be. They could then work out the positions of the sun and stars to navigate by. But the newfangled top didn't catch on because seafarers were useless at spinning it.

But Smeaton's brainwave was the ancestor of gyroscopes found on most ships and planes today.

Foucault's invention – the gyroscope – works like a series of tops. They balance on one another and always stay upright. And this is ideal if you want to steer a steady course. Amazingly, your bike wheels work in much the same way. When they spin round the bike is much less likely tip over than when it's stationary. Scientists call this "precession". Something to think about next time you go for a precession on your bike.

BET YOU NEVER KNEW!

The tighter your circle of spin, the faster you go. That's why ice-skaters pull in their arms to spin faster. It's the law of conservation of angular momentum again. Because the circle of spin is smaller, they go round quicker. This fact also explains why water speeds up near the centre of a whirlpool. You can check this fact by watching the dregs of your washing-up gurgle down the plug hole. And if this isn't your idea of fun you'd better dive into the next chapter. You'll soon get your bounce back.

BAKED BEAN

PEA IS SPINNING FASTER THAN THE BAKED BEAN

BOUNCING BACK

What's always "around" for a game and doesn't mind a good kicking? No, not your sports teacher. It's a *ball.* And oddly enough balls do other forceful things. Like rolling and spinning and bouncing. Here are a few facts to bounce off your friends.

Fatal forces fact file

Name: Bouncing

The basic facts: When a rubber ball hits the floor, the springy coiled rubber molecules that make up the ball are all squashed together. They soak up the energy of the impact and then bounce out again – making the ball bounce.

The horrible details: The first chewing gum was made of chicle, a type of tree sap. American scientists tried to make the chicle into a type of rubber but it wasn't bouncy enough. So they just chewed the problem over, or rather chewed the chicle.

KEEP YOUR EYE ON THE BALL

When a ball flies through the air, strange things start to happen. Scientists have put loads of effort into working out what these mysterious effects are.

Fatal forces fact file

Name:	Flying balls
The basic facts:	When you throw or kick a ball, friction with the air causes drag and this slows the ball. At the same time it's hit by turbulence. That's when spinning masses of air form around the ball and give it a bumpy ride.
The horrible details:	A baseball can be pitched at 90 mph. That's fatally fast for anyone in the way without protective gear.

Any old scientist will tell you that ball games involve forces. So we invited a tame scientist along to show you how science can help you improve at sports such as tennis. According to the scientist you don't need to work up a sweat. All you need is a few brain cells and a small computer. *Oh, yeah?*

THE SCIENTIST'S GUIDE TO TENNIS

Tennis-ball seams are the same on each side. This means equal amounts of air turbulence. So the ball flies straight. That's quite a velocity. Slice the racket downwards and you'll get back-spin. The ball tumbles backwards as it flies forwards. This drags air over it. As this air speeds up, the pressure above the ball drops and the greater air pressure under the ball raises it. We call this effect lift.

RACKET SLICES DOWNWARDS CREATING BACKSPIN ON BALL

DIDN'T THINK IT WOULD 'LIFT' THAT HIGH!

BALL 'LIFTS' AS BACKSPIN CREATES LESS AIR PRESSURE ABOVE BALL AND GREATER PRESSURE BELOW

Top spin is the opposite. Strike the ball upwards and the ball tumbles forwards as it flies forwards. This drags air under the ball. And as it speeds up the pressure drops and the ball is pushed lower and it bounces faster.

RACKET MOVES UPWARDS CREATING TOP SPIN.

BALL BOUNCES FASTER AS TOPSPIN CREATES MORE AIR PRESSURE ABOVE THE BALL AND LESS BELOW

DIDN'T THINK IT WOULD BOUNCE THAT FAST!

If you hit the ball a glancing blow it bounces extra slowly when it hits the ground. So it's even easier to whack.

PAINLESS PADDING

If you find games a pain in the sports bag maybe you need a bit more protection. Here are a few bits and pieces of equipment designed to help you play safe.

- Cushioned shoulder padding and shin pads as worn by American footballers.
- Boxer's gum shield. Stops teeth from being knocked out of their sockets.
- Protective helmet worn by American footballers. Its dome shape spreads the force of a blow over the whole helmet. It stops the head from getting squashed.
- Cricketer's box to protect the vulnerable bits. Very useful – cricket balls travel at 100 mph.

WITH → BOX

HOWZAT!

PAINFUL!

WITHOUT ↗ BOX

HAVING A BALL

1 The first balls were made by the Romans from bits of dead animal skin stitched together and filled with air. Later on, in the Middle Ages, balls were made from pigs' bladders filled with air. Yuck – who had to blow them up?

IMPORTANT!
REMEMBER TO EMPTY THE BLADDER FIRST

2 The first golf balls were leather bags packed with boiled chicken's feathers. Bet that made the feathers fly. The balls flew very well until it rained when they soon got waterlogged and split. Covering the players in grotty old feathers.

3 In the 1850s someone had the idea of making golf balls out of rubbery tree sap. But they didn't fly as straight as the old balls until they became scratched and worn. Then they flew really well.

4 So what was going on? Turned out the rough surface of the golf ball trapped tiny pockets of air. The turbulent air flowed around the trapped air and this actually gave a smoother, quicker flight. And that's why modern golf balls have little dimples.

5 Cricket balls also do strange things as they fly through the air. Normally the ball just spins horizontally. But at speed, air turbulence makes the ball swerve if the edge of the ball's seam is smooth. That's why some cricketers polish the ball by rubbing it on their trousers.

6 At speeds of 99 km per hour (62 mph) plus, the ball can swerve even more. Especially if the edge of the seam is rough. And that's why some cricketers rub dirt into the ball. But don't do this in your games lesson – it's called cheating.

7 The ball used in rugby and American football has pointed ends. If it's tumbling forward it can bounce oddly. Sometimes it bounces high, sometimes low.

8 This makes it tricky to pick up. And dangerous too unless you enjoy twenty giant people jumping on your head. The good news is that the ball is easier to throw. Pitch it with one end pointing forwards and it'll spin horizontally like an over-sized bullet. This means you can easily get rid of it before you get flattened. It's safer than just standing and juggling the ball…

DARE YOU DISCOVER … HOW TO JUGGLE?

Juggling is a great way to see how forces affect balls in the air. Tell your gullible folks you're doing your homework. Then you can have a bit of fun.

You will need:

• Yourself • Something to juggle with. Three balls small enough to fit in your hands would be good. Or you could try rolled up socks • Plenty of space • A mirror

Safety note: When you are learning to juggle try to resist the urge to use your granny's priceless antiques, food (especially at meal-times), and living creatures such as hamsters, goldfish, small brothers and sisters, etc.

1 Stand in front of a mirror with your elbows tucked close to your body and your hands level with your waist. Place your legs apart with your knees slightly bent. Easy, isn't it? Are you ready?

ADOPT A CONFIDENT AND RELAXED EXPRESSION

REMAIN CALM AND STILL

2 Take a deep breath and let it out slowly. That's right – relax. Now without looking at your hands … throw the ball gently up and over your head. Notice how it falls in an arc under the influence of gravity just like the cannonballs Galileo studied – remember? Catch the ball in the palm of your other hand. Keep your eyes on the top part of the ball's flight. OK – that's the easy bit.

3 Now it gets a bit harder. Juggling with two balls takes a bit of practice. Throw one ball up as before. When the ball is just about to drop, throw your second ball up from the other hand. Ideally the second ball should pass just under the first ball.

4 OK, this takes practice. Better practise now to get it right.

5 This is where it gets *really* hard. Three balls. Sure you want to try? OK. Hold two balls in one hand and one in the other. Repeat Step 3.

6 Now here's the clever bit. When ball 2 is just about to drop throw ball 3 up and try to get it to pass under ball 2. Meanwhile catch ball 1 and throw it up just when ball 3 is about to drop. Easy!

7 Fantastic, keep going!

And while you're doing this, here are some interesting facts to juggle with.

1 It's REALLY difficult to juggle with more than 12 objects. But it can be done – in 2013 British youngster Alex Barron juggled 13 beanbags.

2 Kara, a nineteenth-century German performer used to juggle with his hat, lighted cigar, gloves, newspaper, matches and a coffee cup. Don't try this at home … or at school.

3 It's also possible to juggle with your feet. As long as their back is supported, the performer can juggle quite weighty objects including a small child. And this is something you shouldn't try either!

They've even invented a juggling machine. People can enjoy the fun of juggling without ever having to learn for themselves. That's typical of us humans. Always inventing machines to get out of hard work. There are loads more mighty machines that use forces to do work. Listen hard and you'll hear them grinding up their gears for the next chapter...

MIGHTY MACHINES

A machine is a way of using a force in the right place to get a job done with less effort. Good idea. So why, after 10,000 years of science and invention, is there no machine for doing homework? Anyway, to make a mighty machine all you need is a collection of effort-saving levers, pulleys and gears.

FATAL EXPRESSIONS

ARGH! ROTATIONAL INERTIA – I NEED MORE TORQUE!

Should you call a doctor?

No – a mechanic. The scientist can't loosen a nut. Torque is the word scientists use to describe the turning force you produce using a spanner. Rotational inertia is the resistance of the nut to being turned. And spanners are good for doing this job because they work like levers, as you'll see.

LOVELY LEVERS

A lever is a pole that you use to lever something up or push or pull something around. Either way the lever rests on a point known as the fulcrum. Levers work because the most effective turning force is at right angles to the thing you want to move. So levers help you do more work for less effort. Lovely!

DARE YOU DISCOVER ... HOW A LEVER WORKS?

You will need:

• Yourself • A door

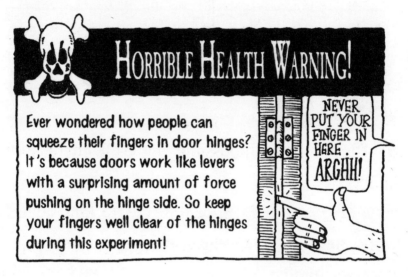

HORRIBLE HEALTH WARNING!

Ever wondered how people can squeeze their fingers in door hinges? It's because doors work like levers with a surprising amount of force pushing on the hinge side. So keep your fingers well clear of the hinges during this experiment!

NEVER PUT YOUR FINGER IN HERE ... ARGHH!

What you do:

1 Open the door slightly. Make sure no one charges through the door.

2 Stand outside the door and try to push it by pressing with one finger 2 cm from the hinges.

3 Now press with the same finger 2 cm from the opposite side to the hinges.

NEAR THE HINGES

AWAY FROM THE HINGES

Which is easier?

a) They're both impossible and you got a sore finger.

b) It's easier to push the door near the hinges.

c) It's easier to push the door further away from the hinges.

ANSWER

c) The door works like a lever with the hinges as the fulcrum. The further away from the fulcrum you press, the more forceful your push is. Nowadays you'll find levers everywhere. From typewriters to tin openers and from scissors to see-saws.

BET YOU NEVER KNEW!

You've got levers in your body. This interesting fact was discovered by the Italian artist and scientist Leonardo da Vinci (1452–1519).

Leonardo was cutting up human arms and legs in a bid to find how they worked. He discovered that muscles pulled the bones in much the same way as you pull a lever to move an object. He was so excited by this discovery that he even made a working model leg using copper wires and bits of real human bones. Then he could see it in action.

TEACHER'S TEA-BREAK TEASER

This playground puzzle spells break-time bafflement for your teacher. Two children are playing on a see-saw. If the little child jumps off she might get hurt. If the big child gets off he'll get a nasty injury as the see-saw swings up under the weight of the smaller child.

WHAT'S TO BE DONE?

FULCRUM

The see-saw acts like a lever – that's why it's so good at lifting children off the ground. The larger child's weight pushes with greater force on his end of the see-saw. If he moves towards the fulcrum, the lever would be less effective at lifting the small child. As a result she would be gently lowered to the ground. Why not try this experiment on your friends?

POWERFUL PULLEYS

Another method of lifting heavy weights off the ground – including large children – is the pulley. Basically it's a wheel hung off the ground with a rope passing over it. This re-directs force. So you can pull on the rope and lift something tied to the other end of the rope.

Add another wheel to the first one and it's even easier. By pulling the rope a longer distance you spread the effort so it seems easier to lift the load.

Nowadays you'll find pulleys on cranes and lifts. So whom do we have to thank for this amazing invention? It was a Greek genius – Archimedes (c.287–c.212 BC).

A LOVELY LITTLE MOVER

Archimedes had a little problem. His relative, Hieron, had asked him to pull a full-sized ship down a beach and out to sea – without help! Now most of us would tell the brother-in-law to jump in a vat of custard and go back to watching the telly. But Archimedes couldn't say that.

Unfortunately, Hieron was the local king – Hieron II of Syracuse to be exact. And you don't refuse royalty even if

170

they are family. Besides, Archimedes was an all-round genius. He was supposed to know these things. He'd already worked out the maths of levers and boasted that with a long enough lever he could lift the world. Hieron thought his brainy relative should be taught a lesson. So he deliberately set him an impossible task.

Archimedes scratched his balding head and chewed his lip. All that night he worked on mathematical plans. And eventually he hit on a solution. An answer so stunningly original, so forceful and amazing that no one had ever thought of it before. A new machine. Meanwhile, hundreds of grim-faced guards grunted and groaned as they hauled the ship up the beach. Hieron ordered them to load the ship with cargo and told some of them to wait on board.

Archimedes and a few assistants spent the next few hours setting up the machine. History doesn't record what it looked like. But it must have been a series of pulleys standing on wooden frames with the rope tied securely to the ship. When all was ready Archimedes gripped the free end of the rope. He looked rather thin and weedy. Hieron couldn't resist a quiet chuckle as Archimedes rolled up his sleeves and tugged on the rope.

But then the ship slid smoothly down the beach. It moved with eerie ease as if it was sailing on a calm sea. Archimedes' machine was a lovely little mover. The watching crowds gasped in disbelief. The people on the ship looked stunned and Hieron nearly had a heart attack. If he hadn't seen it with his own eyes the king would have accused his brainy relative of pulley-ing his leg.

GRINDING GEARS

No one knows who invented gears but the Romans certainly used them. They're interlocking toothed wheels that pass on force and they have odd sounding names that wouldn't be out of place in an ancient torture chamber. Names such as "bevels", "rack and pinion", "spurs" and "worms". They all work the same way. A smaller wheel that turns quickly and a larger wheel that turns more slowly.

INTERLOCKING TEETH

LARGE WHEEL TURNS SLOWLY

SMALL WHEEL TURNS FAST

SCIENTIST'S TEETH

Gears control the speed and direction of the turning force you put in. Take your bicycle gears, for example. The gear wheels on your bike have fewer teeth than the chain wheel. So the gear wheels turn faster and they make your rear bike wheel turn faster than you pedal. So it does you a really good turn.

GEAR WHEELS

GASP! WHEEZE!

GEAR MECHANISM MOVES CHAIN ONTO DIFFERENT-SIZED GEAR WHEELS

CHAIN WHEEL

The bicycle was such a good idea that nineteenth-century inventors began to peddle their own pedal-powered machines. Which of these are too silly to be true?

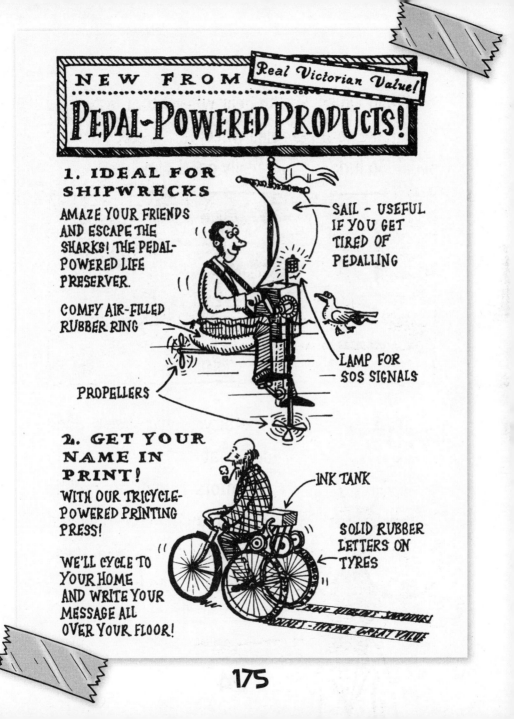

NEW FROM

Real Victorian Value!

PEDAL-POWERED PRODUCTS!

1. IDEAL FOR SHIPWRECKS

AMAZE YOUR FRIENDS AND ESCAPE THE SHARKS! THE PEDAL-POWERED LIFE PRESERVER.

COMFY AIR-FILLED RUBBER RING

PROPELLERS

SAIL - USEFUL IF YOU GET TIRED OF PEDALLING

LAMP FOR SOS SIGNALS

2. GET YOUR NAME IN PRINT!

WITH OUR TRICYCLE-POWERED PRINTING PRESS!

WE'LL CYCLE TO YOUR HOME AND WRITE YOUR MESSAGE ALL OVER YOUR FLOOR!

INK TANK

SOLID RUBBER LETTERS ON TYRES

3. DON'T MISS OUR BUS!

NO MORE SCHOOL BUS BREAKDOWNS. TRY THE NEW PEDAL-POWERED SCHOOL BUS. SPECIAL PEDALS UNDER THE SEATS LINKED TO A ROTATING CRANKSHAFT POWER THE BUS AT 35KM PER HOUR (22 MPH).

"GETS THE KIDS TO SCHOOL ON TIME AND KEEPS THEM FIT."
I. FLOGGEM (HEADMASTER)

4. TIRED OUT?

RELAX UNDER OUR DELIGHTFUL PEDAL-POWERED COLD SHOWER!

ALL THE REFRESHING DELIGHTS OF GETTING CAUGHT IN THE RAIN WHILE ON YOUR BIKE!

A NEW AND EXCITING FORM OF EXERCISE THAT LEAVES YOU FEELING FRESH AND FIT

PEDAL YOUR WAY TO A CLEAN BODY!

RINSE YOUR SWEAT AWAY

PEDAL ACTION PUMPS WATER UP PIPE AND OUT OF THE SHOWER HEAD

MARVELLOUS MIGHTY MACHINES

A complicated machine is simply lots of simple machines joined together. Easy. Just a load of old screws, pulleys, levers, gears, wheels, axles, chains, transmission shafts and springs that you just happen to find lying about in the garage. Throw them all together and everything should go like clockwork.

From bikes and gears it's a small step to steam engines, petrol engines, trains, buses, cars and planes. Just think. If it wasn't for forces, they wouldn't be able to force you to go to school. Terrible. Still, you can relax at home, can't you? No need to worry about forces in there? Safe as houses and all that ... er – well, actually, forces *can* be fatal for buildings, too. The next chapter will really shake you up.

BUILD OR BUST

Fallen down under the influence of gravity, blown down, blown up or just shaken about. Yep. Forces are fatal for buildings, too.

BODGE-IT BUILDINGS

Some buildings stand for hundreds of years. Others stand for hundreds of days ... or minutes.

Would you be interested in buying any of these structures?

WAT-ER GREAT BRIDGE!

LONDON BRIDGE, Spanning the River Thames in London on 20 narrow arches (built 1176-1209)

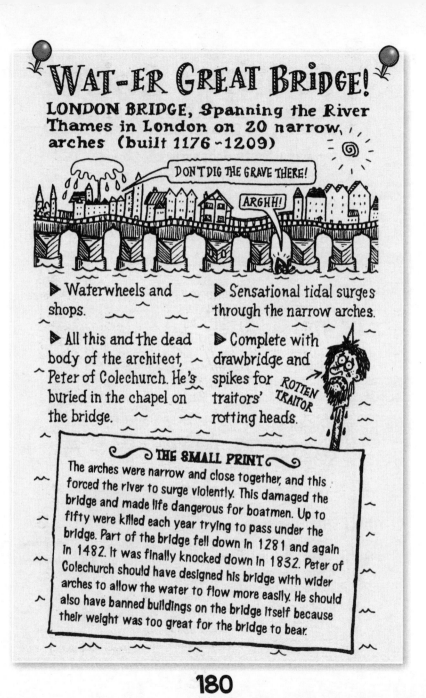

DON'T DIG THE GRAVE THERE!

ARGHH!

▶ Waterwheels and shops.

▶ Sensational tidal surges through the narrow arches.

▶ All this and the dead body of the architect, Peter of Colechurch. He's buried in the chapel on the bridge.

▶ Complete with drawbridge and spikes for traitors' rotting heads.

ROTTEN TRAITOR

THE SMALL PRINT

The arches were narrow and close together, and this forced the river to surge violently. This damaged the bridge and made life dangerous for boatmen. Up to fifty were killed each year trying to pass under the bridge. Part of the bridge fell down in 1281 and again in 1482. It was finally knocked down in 1832. Peter of Colechurch should have designed his bridge with wider arches to allow the water to flow more easily. He should also have banned buildings on the bridge itself because their weight was too great for the bridge to bear.

Go With A Swing!

THE TACOMA NARROWS BRIDGE, Washington State, USA (built 1940)

▶ A graceful lightweight suspension bridge. (That's a bridge supported by cables hung from towers.)

▶ Amazing 853-metre span.

▶ Swings about in the wind for a really exciting crossing.

WIND YOUR WINDOWS UP KIDS

THE SMALL PRINT

The Tacoma Narrows Bridge swayed so violently in the wind that it earned the nickname "Galloping Gertie". People actually felt seasick crossing it. The bridge had to be reinforced to stop the swaying spreading to the towers that held up the cables. But four months later a strong wind twisted the roadway sideways until it collapsed.

GO UNDERCOVER!

THE KEMPER ARENA, Kansas City, USA (built 1973)

▶ Spectacular covered all-weather sports stadium. Keeps that nasty rain off your head.

▶ Winner of an architectural award in 1976.

▶ Cost $23.3 million to build.

THE SMALL PRINT
In 1979 the roof of the Kemper Arena fell in after heavy rain. Engineers believe rainwater collected on the roof making it sag until its supports couldn't take the weight any longer.

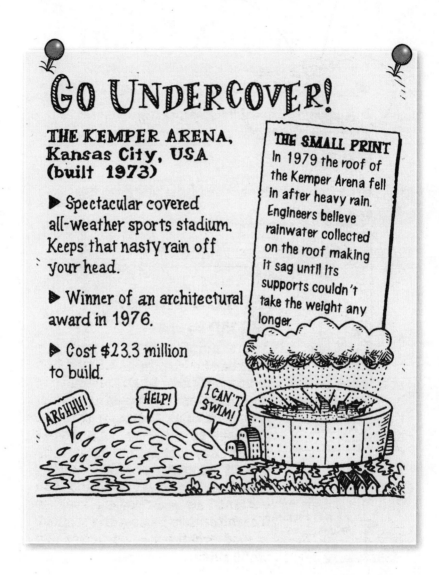

BET YOU NEVER KNEW!

When a building falls down many people can be killed. But when a dam bursts the results can be even more fatal. A dam has to hold back the huge force of water that builds up against it. That's why dams have such thick walls and are often built in a strong arch shape so the water presses the dam into the sides of the valley rather than backwards. But sometimes this isn't enough. In 1975 flooding burst two dams in Henan province in China and 235,000 people were washed away. So you can see how important it is for all architects to be properly trained. If you'd like to be a good architect you'd better pay attention to these simple rules...

BECOME AN ARCHITECT IN SIX EASY LESSONS

LESSON 1: UNDERSTAND THE EFFECT OF FORCES ON YOUR BUILDING

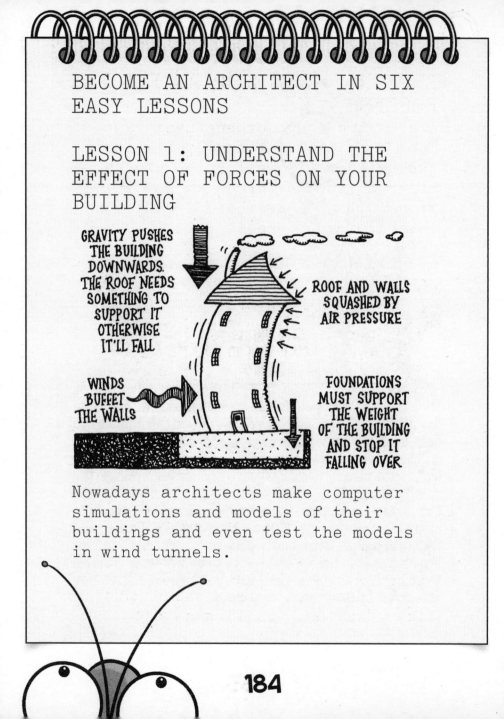

GRAVITY PUSHES THE BUILDING DOWNWARDS. THE ROOF NEEDS SOMETHING TO SUPPORT IT OTHERWISE IT'LL FALL

ROOF AND WALLS SQUASHED BY AIR PRESSURE

WINDS BUFFET THE WALLS

FOUNDATIONS MUST SUPPORT THE WEIGHT OF THE BUILDING AND STOP IT FALLING OVER

Nowadays architects make computer simulations and models of their buildings and even test the models in wind tunnels.

LESSON 2: DEVELOP AN EYE FOR FORCES

A good architect or engineer can look at a building and spot whether the building is well built enough to stand up to the forces on it. Marc Brunel (that's Isambard's dad) once looked at a bridge in Paris and said:

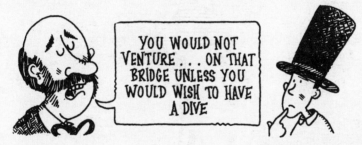

YOU WOULD NOT VENTURE... ON THAT BRIDGE UNLESS YOU WOULD WISH TO HAVE A DIVE

Three days later, the bridge collapsed. Yep, old Marc kept dry and he certainly had a dry sense of humour too.

LESSON 3: PUT IN PROPER FOUNDATIONS

If you've ever tried to carry some tall glasses on a tray one-handed like a waiter, you'll know how tricky it is to balance them. It would help if the glasses were partly buried in a really thick tray. That's how foundations work. The taller the building, the deeper the foundations you need.

Foundations stop the wind from blowing your building over and they support the weight of your building too. Remember Galileo working at Pisa University? In 1173 Pisa's bell tower was built on soft ground with foundations that weren't broad enough to support its weight. Now Pisa University's famous for its learning and the tower's famous for its leaning.

LESSON 4: ALWAYS BUILD YOUR BUILDING THE RIGHT SHAPE

Triangles are a good strong shape. That's why the Egyptian pyramids have lasted 4,700 years. The Eiffel Tower was also made up of a series of triangles and many modern skyscrapers use triangles as the basis of their metal frames.

A column is a good strong shape and ideal for holding up heavy weights. Like the roof, for example. You can use arches to hold up part of the walls. Like columns, arches are great because the harder you push down on them the more they push back. Yes — it's Newton's Third Law again.

Dome shapes are also very strong. But you knew that from reading about American football helmets. An egg shape is also surprisingly strong and can take a weight of 22.7 kg. But don't try leaving an egg on your teacher's chair.

TEACHER WHO WEIGHS MORE THAN 22.7KG (50 lbs)

CRUNCH!

LESSON 5: MAKE SURE YOUR WALLS DON'T FALL DOWN

If you are designing a very tall stone building you may choose to make your walls very thick like an old cathedral or castle — the walls of the Tower of London are more than 4.6 metres thick. So you want to put in larger windows but you know they will weaken your walls. No problem. Try using buttresses to hold your walls up.

Mind you, disasters do happen. In 1989 the Civic Tower in Pavia, Italy, (built 1060) fell with a crash. The cement holding the stones together had slowly crumbled away. Engineers reckoned that the shock waves from years of ringing the bells at the top had brought on the destruction.

If this puts you off building in stone you could use a strong steel frame for your tall building and use lighter materials for your walls. This makes them stronger but the building might sway a bit in windy weather.

LESSON 6: GET YOUR ROOF THE RIGHT SHAPE

Roofs are usually sloping because the curved shape is more difficult to bend. You can prove this by holding a piece of paper in different ways.

HOLD IT LIKE THIS AND IT'S FLOPPY

BUT HOLD THE PAPER LIKE THIS AND IT'S STRAIGHT.

VICIOUS VIBES

One thing that can be very destructive is vibration. Have you ever watched a washing machine shuddering and shaking as it washes and spins the clothes. Perhaps you've bravely laid a finger on the machine and felt the shaking passing up your arms. These are vibrations. And beware. They can be vicious.

TRAPPING YOUR TIE COULD PROVE FATAL...

FATAL EXPRESSIONS

Should you dial 999? No, her car's shuddering with vibrations. Probably because it's so clapped out. Oscillatory motion is in fact what vibrations are called. Oscillations are regularly repeated movements or shaking. The only way to stop them is to "damp them down". No, this doesn't mean chucking water over the car. Still confused? Well, it means using some soft substance to absorb the vibrations and stop the shuddering.

VICIOUS VIBRATION FACTS

Vibrations are particularly vicious in their effects on buildings and bridges. In 1850, 487 soldiers were marching across a suspension bridge in Algiers in Africa. Their heavy boots thudded on the roadway. And soon the whole bridge was shaking with the vibrations. It shook so much that bits fell off it and finally the entire bridge collapsed into the river. Tragically 226 soldiers were killed.

Ever since, soldiers avoid marching in step when they cross a bridge in order not set off the deadly vibrations. That takes a bit of foresight but sometimes it pays to plan the crossing of your bridges before you come to them. Mind you, the most vicious vibrations aren't caused by people – they're caused by the Earth itself.

Every year there are hundreds of earthquakes.

Some of them are fatal for people. Movement of vast rocky areas deep under the ground trigger powerful vibrations in the form of shock waves that can destroy entire cities. The damage is done because shock waves make the walls vibrate so violently that the building falls down. Feeling a little shaky?

DARE YOU DISCOVER ... HOW MUCH YOUR BODY VIBRATES?

You will need:

YOURSELF

LARGE ERASER OR SMALL WEIGHT

30-CM RULER

What you do:

1 Place the eraser on the end of ruler.

2 Grip the opposite end of the ruler by your thumb

and forefinger. Then hold the ruler as close to its end as you can.

3 Stretch out your hand, balancing the eraser on the opposite end of the ruler.

What do you notice?

a) Nothing. I did the test for ten minutes and my hand was steady as a rock.

b) After a few seconds the end of the ruler began to dance around as my arm twitched.

c) I lost my balance and fell over forwards.

ANSWER

b) Your body vibrates constantly as your heart beats and the blood squirts around your body. Your muscles also pulse of their own accord. So your body's vibrations pass along the ruler and make it twitch. If you get answer **a)** try a heavier weight. If you get answer **c)** try a lighter one.

A SMASHING FINALE

Now you've learnt about how forces affect buildings, let's practise using forces to knock one down. An old school will do. Imagine your school has been condemned as an unsafe building. Perhaps all those hundreds of feet stomping up and down the corridors has triggered vicious vibrations that have fatally weakened the building. Now your school must be flattened. No more science lessons – that's really tough. Oh well – here's how to do the demolition job...

1 Make sure that the school is empty of all pupils and there are no teachers lurking in the corners. You wouldn't want to knock the building down on top of them would you?

2 Start off by swinging a heavy steel ball against the walls of your school. The ball transfers its momentum to the wall as it crashes into it. Cement is dislodged from the bricks and the wall falls down.

3 If you don't have a steel ball you'll have to smash the walls with a sledgehammer. This has the same effect but it's far slower and much harder work.

4 Some buildings have pre-stressed concrete beams. These are concrete beams with steel wires running through them. The wires are held tight by the weight of the building's upper floors. Be careful if your school has these beams. When you knock down the upper floors, the wires in the lower floor's beams aren't held tight any more. So they go *ping* and the entire building crashes down around your ears.

PING!

Alternatively you could try one of these demolition methods.

Method 1.
Explosives

In a hurry? Want to knock your school down before science class on Monday? You could blow it up. Place explosive charges around the building and weaken the supporting beams so they collapse easily. Set off the explosives and wait for the dust to clear!

Method 2.
Hands

If you can't blow up your school, try using your bare hands instead. A karate blow is forceful enough to break bricks. In 1994 15 karate experts demolished a seven-room house in Saskatchewan, Canada using only their bare feet and hands.

MAY THE FORCES BE WITH YOU

Forces were around long before we got here. And although we try to use forces – in the end we can't control them. We can only forecast what forces might do to new buildings or cars. And although designers make fatal mistakes, these embarrassing slip-ups are thankfully rare.

THE DESIGN IS FINE ~ YOU'VE GOT THE PLANS UPSIDE DOWN

Meanwhile, physicists are making more brain-boggling discoveries about forces. Before Galileo and Newton, no one knew how forces worked. Today we know more about them than ever. And because forces affect so much of our world, they pop up in every area of scientific knowledge.

Take atoms, for example. Scientists are probing how forces hold an atom together. (Atoms are the tiny bits of matter that make up everything in the universe.) The trick is to smash the atoms together in awesome machines called accelerators tens of kilometres long. Then you sift the debris for clues. If you're a scientist it sometimes pays to think small, ha ha.

Forces also come into space travel. To plan a little trip around the solar system you need to know how a planet's gravity will pull your craft. And you need to be sure what happens when you whizz round a planet and zoom off into the depths of space. So you'll be needing an advanced computer to cope with the necessary maths.

Other physicists are looking into how gravity itself works. Are there really tiny things, even smaller than atoms, called gravitons that are somehow involved? And once scientists have found this out, could they perhaps defeat gravity and make planes that hover effortlessly in the air?

And even if we don't crack this one – there's always something new. Like a really wacky new sport. Take sky-surfing, for example. To do this you have to be seriously off your trolley. It involves jumping from an aeroplane strapped to a board. You enjoy some mid-air acrobatics before your parachute opens – assuming it does.

But one thing is certain – humans will go on pushing forces to their limits and scientists will go on studying how forces work. After all there may be limits to our knowledge, but our curiosity knows no bounds. Yep. You're forced to admit it. Forces are horribly intriguing. Fatally fascinating. But that's Horrible Science for you!

HORRIBLE INDEX